TABLE OF CONTENTS

Image by Michael Ayers.

PROFESSIONAL

DIGITAL IMAGING

FOR WEDDING AND PORTRAIT PHOTOGRAPHERS

PATRICK RICE

AMHERST MEDIA, INC. ■ BUFFALO, NY

Front cover photos: Barbara Rice (large photo) and Patrick Rice (insets).
Back cover photos: Patrick Rice (top photo) and Barbara Rice (bottom photo).

Published by:
Amherst Media, Inc.
P.O. Box 586
Buffalo, N.Y. 14226
Fax: 716-874-4508
www.AmherstMedia.com

Publisher: Craig Alesse
Senior Editor/Production Manager: Michelle Grant
Assistant Editor: Barbara A. Lynch-Johnt

ISBN: 1-58428-128-6
Library of Congress Card Catalog Number: 2003112484

Printed in Korea.
10 9 8 7 6 5 4 3 2 1

Notice of Disclaimer: The information contained in this book is based on the author's experience and opinions. The author and publisher will not be held liable for the use or misuse of the information in this book.

Image by Patrick Rice.

ABOUT THE AUTHOR AND CONTRIBUTORS

◻ ABOUT THE AUTHOR

Patrick Rice holds the PPA (Professional Photographers of America) Master of Photography and Photographic Craftsman degrees, as well as all five levels of Masters degrees from WPPI (Wedding and Portrait Photographers International). He regularly serves as a juror in both regional and national print competitions for both PPA and WPPI. In addition to achieving countless Best of Show honors, he was WPPI's Grand Award winner in the portrait category in 1997. In the same year, one of his wedding images received a perfect score of 100 in WPPI's Awards of Excellence Print Competition. He has accumulated seven Court of Honor Awards in the Wedding category at the Mideast States Regional Print Competition, and in 2001 received two Fuji Masterpiece Awards.

Patrick is also a much sought-after speaker, whose presentations on infrared wedding photography at national photography conferences attract standing-room-only crowds. He is also a regular contributor to *Rangefinder* and other professional photography magazines.

With Barbara Rice and Travis Hill, Patrick is the co-author of *Infrared Wedding Photography* (Amherst Media, 2000). He is also the author of *The Professional Photographer's Guide to Success in Print Competition* (Amherst Media, 2003).

◻ CONTRIBUTORS

As you read through this book, you'll notice that many of the chapters contain sections called "A Professional Perspective." These are articles by other professional photographers and digital imagers who were generous enough to contribute their thoughts on the challenges (and rewards) of professional digital photography. Because every studio, market, and photographer is different, these sections provide valuable insights and ideas for working with digital and can help to round out your knowledge of the subject. The following individuals have contributed their words and images:

PENNY ADAMS—Penny Adams graduated with honors from the Dawson Institute of Photography in Montreal, Canada, and has photographed families, weddings, and other events throughout the United States and Canada. In addition to being the owner and operator of Adler House Photography, she has been honored to serve on the Board of Directors for the Professional Photographers of Ohio (PPO) and the Professional Photographers of Central Ohio. As a member of PPO, Penny recently received the Ohio Fuji Masterpiece award for wedding photography.

MICHAEL AYERS—The recipient of two Master of Photography degrees and the United Nations Leadership Award, Michael Ayers has made a career of giving back to the photographic industry. He has invented album designs and construction concepts, authored countless articles and books, and has lectured to more than 25,000 photographers worldwide. To view samples from Michael's work, visit: www.TheAyers.com.

MICHAEL BELL—Michael Bell received his Master of Photography and Photographic Craftsman degrees in 1998, and was the first photographer to receive both degrees simultaneously. He received his Certified Professional Photographer status from PPA. Mike has also achieved great success in print competition, with two of his prints having been accepted into PPA's Loan Collection. His work has also been featured in *Rangefinder* and *Storytellers* magazines.

MARK BOHLAND—Mark Bohland is a Certified Professional Photographer and has received the

Photographic Craftsman degree from PPA. His award-winning images have been widely published. He has photographed weddings as well as child and family portraits since 1978, and has a unique way of approaching a portrait. "Most people have a picture taken and then decide whether or not they like it, and where it will go in their home. I think that's really a backwards way of looking at artistic portraiture," says Bohland. "The purpose of a portrait is to reveal something of the spirit of the subject. A truly artistic portrait begins in the mind, and is the result of a collaboration between the artist and the subject. A portrait is actually created before the camera even clicks. Both the subject and the artist should know enough about what the finished portrait will look like to know ahead of time that they will like it."

RON BURGESS—After a twenty-year career as a registered nurse, Ron Burgess completed his course of study with the New York Institute of Photography. In 1991 he opened his own studio, specializing in on-location photography and other photography-related services. His images have won awards in both national and regional print competitions.

MICHEAL DWYER—Micheal Dwyer is president and "chief bean" of MDP, Inc., which operates three studios with a staff of nine in Arlington, Omaha, and Lincoln, NB. Together, they photograph over 1100 sessions a year—and since 1998, virtually all of them have been without film. Micheal is a past member of the board of directors of Professional Photographers of Nebraska, a charter member of the advisory panel of Burrell Professional Labs, and Presidential Circle member and chairman of the Midwest Digital Imaging Conference. He received his Photographic Craftsman degree from PPA in 1999 and is the author of *Preparing for the Digital Revolution* (Marathon Press, 2000). Micheal is also a nationally registered emergency medical technician and captain of the Arlington Rescue Squad; he serves as his county's emergency management director.

RICK FERRO and DEBORAH LYNN FERRO— Rick Ferro holds a Master of Photography degree from PPA and is one of the nation's leading wedding photographers. In 1993, Walt Disney World approached Rick to create a wedding photography department. He became senior wedding photographer for Disney—and Walt Disney World became the world's most sought-after wedding destination. Rick went on to serve as a photographer for ABC's *Weddings of a Lifetime* and for weddings on *Live with Regis & Kathy Lee*. Rick is the author of *Wedding Photography: Creative Techniques for Lighting and Posing* (Amherst Media, 1999) and is a popular speaker at national photography conventions. His images have been honored with inclusion in the Loan Collection and Showcase Collection, and have also earned the Kodak Master Gallery Award.

After winning several awards as an active amateur photographer and photography student, Deborah Lynn Ferro opened her own studio in 1996. Specializing in portrait photography and digital artistry, her work attracted clients such as Pillsbury and Target. Now the wife and business partner of Rick Ferro, Deborah continues to stay on top of the trends in the market and teach her skills to photographers around the country. With Rick, Deborah is the co-author of *Wedding Photography with Adobe Photoshop* (Amherst Media, 2003).

SCOTT GLOGER—Scott Gloger has been a photographer practically his whole life. His father, Myron Gloger, started his first studio in the 1940s, so Scott was always around photography. Since taking over the helm at Myron Photographic Excellence in Beachwood, OH, Scott's work has won him numerous awards—including the Fuji Masterpiece Award. Scott was also named Retoucher of the Year by the Photographic Art Specialists of Ohio. Scott has earned the Photographic Craftsman and Certified Professional Photographer degrees from PPA. His service to the profession includes being elected president of the Akron Society of Professional Photographers and serving on the board of trustees of PPO.

BERNARD GRATZ—Bernard Gratz owns and operates Portraits by Bernard in Dover, OH. A professional photographer for over thirty years, Bernard holds the Photographic Craftsman degree from PPA and has served several years as an elected councillor to that association. He is a past president of the Akron Society of Professional Photographers, has served on the board of trustees for PPO for more than twenty years, and is a past chairman of that association.

JEFF and KATHLEEN HAWKINS—Jeff Hawkins has been a professional photographer for over twenty years. In addition to serving as the public relations director of the Wedding Professionals of Central Florida and on the board of directors of the Professional Photographers Society of Central Florida, Jeff has won numerous awards in national print competitions and is a sought-after lecturer on marketing and digital photography.

Kathleen Hawkins is the author of *The Bride's Guide to Wedding Photography: How to Get the Wedding Photography of Your Dreams* (Amherst Media, 2003) and *Digital Photography for Children's and Family Portraiture* (Amherst Media, 2003). In addition to overseeing the operation of Jeff Hawkins Photography, Kathleen is a marketing and sales consultant for photographers in Florida and is sponsored by Art Leather and Gross National Product. She conducts private consultations and leads workshops at photography conventions worldwide, educating photographers on the products and services needed to create a successful business and heirloom products for their clients.

Together with her husband Jeff, she is the coauthor of *Professional Marketing & Selling Techniques for Wedding Photographers* and *Professional Techniques for Digital Wedding Photography* (both from Amherst Media).

TRAVIS HILL—Travis Hill holds PPA's Master of Photography and Photographic Craftsman degrees, and was one of the association's youngest recipients of these high honors. He also holds the Accolade of Lifetime Photographic Achievement from Wedding and Portrait Photographers International (WPPI). He has earned the designation of Certified Professional Photographer from both PPA and PPO. In addition to having one of his images accepted in the PPA Traveling Loan Collection, he has collected four Court of Honor Awards for his wedding photography. Travis has lectured extensively with his parents on wedding and infrared photography. He was a speaker at the PPA Annual Convention in 1999 and WPPI in 2003 and has lectured to audiences both large and small across the country. Travis coauthored the book *Infrared Wedding Photography* (Amherst Media, 2000).

KEN HOLIDA—Ken Holida is an award-winning professional photographer. Ken operates Holiday Photography in Willard, OH, and has over twenty years experience in wedding and portrait imaging. He holds the Master of Photography degree from PPA and earned the distinction of Certified Professional Photographer from both PPA and PPO. Ken is very active in photographic organizations; he served as the president of PPO and as an elected councilor to PPA.

JACOB JAKUSZEIT—Jacob Jakuszeit has been in love with photography for many years. This passion for imaging led him to Rice Photography, where he has worked as a wedding photographer for the past four years. Having photographed his first wedding solo at age sixteen, Jacob has always stepped up and excelled. Graduating at the top of his class from North Olmstead High School, Jacob is also an Eagle Scout. Jacob went on to study photography at Baldwin Wallace College, and his work has won awards in numerous photographic competitions. His grasp of digital imaging and photojournalistic style make him an excellent image-maker.

ROBERT KUNESH—Robert is an art teacher, photographer, and co-owner of Studio K Photography and SKP Photo Lab in Willoughby, OH. Since receiving his first print merit in 1997, Robert has accumulated thirty-one additional merits in both regular and digital competition in the PPA. Five of his images have been chosen for the PPA Loan Collection, and three have been placed in the PPA Showcase book. He has also earned a Kodak Gallery Award, a Fuji Masterpiece Award, three Court Of Honor awards, as well as over 100 Accolades (WPPI merits) since joining in 1998.

MICHELLE PERKINS—Michelle Perkins is a professional writer and digital photo retoucher specializing in wedding, portrait, and architectural imaging. She has written for *PC Photo*, and is the author of *Traditional Photographic Effects with Adobe® Photoshop®*, *Beginner's Guide to Adobe® Photoshop®*, and *Color Correction and Enhancement with Adobe® Photoshop®*, all available from Amherst Media.

BARBARA RICE—Barbara Rice has had an extensive professional photography career that has allowed her to work for studios in four states over the past twenty-six years. She received her formal photographic education from the Rhode Island School of Photography, and has gone on to earn numerous professional degrees, including PPA's Master of Photography and Photographic Craftsman Degrees. In addition, she holds the Accolade of Lifetime Photographic Excellence and Honorary Accolade of Lifetime Photographic Excellence Degrees from WPPI. Barbara has received numerous awards in WPPI print competitions, and she had the highest-scoring print in the entire 1998 WPPI Award of Excellence Competition—a score of 99! Her creative wedding albums have received the Fuji Masterpiece Award, and one was accepted into the PPA Loan Collection. Barbara coauthored the book *Infrared Wedding Photography* (Amherst Media, 2000).

JEFF SMITH—Jeff Smith is a professional photographer who operates two studios specializing in senior portrait photography. A regular contributor to numerous magazines on professional photography, Jeff is also the author of *Outdoor and Location Portrait Photography, Corrective Lighting and Posing Techniques for Portrait Photography, Professional Digital Portrait Photography,* and *Success in Portrait Photography,* all from Amherst Media.

CHAD TSOUFIOU—Chad Tsoufiou is one of the brightest young stars in the field of wedding photography. With nearly ten years' experience taking pictures, his talents have matured very quickly. His formal training in photography began at Lake High School in Hartville, OH. From there, Chad went on to study photography at Kent State University. Chad excelled at Kent, being named to the Dean's list four times. He graduated with a bachelors degree in photo illustration. Chad has won several awards for his photography throughout the years, and has worked as both a portrait and commercial photographer. Working both as the primary and secondary (documentary) photographer at Rice Photography, Chad has developed a unique ability to capture the feelings and emotions of a wedding day.

ROBERT WILLIAMS—Robert Williams runs Robert Williams Photography in Tallmadge, OH. His portrait and wedding images have won numerous awards in local, state, and national competitions. Robert holds a Master of Photography degree from PPA. He has earned the Certified Professional Photographer degree from PPO, and also earned that association's Advanced Award Medallion. Robert is a past chairman of the Ohio Certified Professional Photographers Commission, and a past president of Professional Photographers of Ohio.

TONY ZIMCOSKY—Anthony (Tony) Zimcosky, a native of Cleveland, OH, is committed to recording the true feelings and emotions of each bride and groom he photographs. What began as a hobby over twenty-six years ago has now become his passion. Whether he is choosing the perfect location for a romantic image or posing the bridal party to make everyone look their best, Tony's concern for excellence and his enthusiasm for creating the highest quality photos is evident. His images have won numerous awards in photographic competitions, and he is very close to completing all of the requirements for WPPI's Accolade of Photographic Mastery degree.

GETTING STARTED

Having spoken to dozens of photographers from across the nation, it is interesting to find that most digital photographers got started in the same way. Like anything in photography, you learn best by doing. I recommend that any photographer interested in digital photography begin by purchasing an inexpensive digital camera and starting to create digital images. Besides gaining valuable experience on image capture, the photographer will begin to understand all of the other areas related to digital—storage media, image output, workflow, image manipulation, etc.

We began by purchasing a "prosumer" digital camera several years ago and just started taking pictures. This first camera helped us get used to working with digital and with image files in the computer. As our confidence in digital cameras increased, we invested in increasingly better models, leading to our first professional digital SLR—the Canon D30. The image quality from the D30 really proved to us that the time was right to switch to digital image capture. We immediately began photographing all of our studio work with the D30. The results were incredible! We then began using the D30 for engagement sessions and when photographing high-school seniors outdoors. Again, the results surpassed our expectations.

Our last holdout for film was wedding photography. We began using our D30s (we now had three of them) on weddings along with the film cameras. We were actually providing film capture for the client and digital capture just for us. We did this to not only give us confidence in using digital cameras in many diverse lighting situations, but also to make sure we could handle the change in the workflow that digital imaging dictates.

As it turned out, with countless labs, camera stores, and even department stores adding Fuji Frontier digital printers, and the introduction of software programs like Fuji's StudioMaster PRO, the transition to digital image capture became an easy one. As a result, we have been working exclusively with digital since 2001.

As our confidence in digital cameras increased, we invested in better digital cameras.

■ A PROFESSIONAL PERSPECTIVE

Digital Photography: How it All Started for Me, by Penny Adams
Over the past four years we've had the opportunity to witness a massive upheaval in the photography industry: the ushering in of the mainstream digital era. When

digital photography was in its infancy, I, like most photographers, started to learn about it in bits and pieces through trade publications and at seminars. I'd often discuss what I had learned with my husband, who works in the software industry. He recognized the change that was about to encompass photography and encouraged me to explore the options that were becoming available in digital photography.

First Impressions. I quickly learned that "digital" meant much more than capturing images with a digital camera. It encompassed all aspects of computerized imagery, such as the scanning of negatives and prints and the manipulation of these using programs like Adobe® Photoshop®. This provided new opportunities for the artistic manipulation of images, including immediate retouching and new ways to plan albums.

It also provided new ways to work with customers, letting us do presentations on big-screen televisions or by connecting a projector to a computer. This improved the interaction with customers, letting them participate in album planning more actively, or letting them see what a large-size wall portrait would look like. It has also made it possible to work remotely with customers, letting a woman in Europe see and purchase the portraits from her granddaughter's wedding, or the results of a photography session with her newborn grandchild.

Image by Penny Adams.

The introduction of pixels into our industry was originally met with skepticism and, by many, disdain. The belief was that the cost of entry into digital photography, coupled with the low quality of the digital images (compared to film capture), would prohibit this technology from becoming mainstream. There were, of course, early adapters, all enthusiastic, some quite vocal. While they were very astute in their observations, their initial enthusiasm caused some friction with the traditional, conservative base of photographers.

Digital Presentation Systems. I started incorporating digital products into my wedding and portrait business slowly. I initially bought a Tamron Fotovix as a mechanism to facilitate the transition to a proofless operation by displaying images scanned at the studio. While this added options in dealing with customers, it also added additional time to the overall operations. When ProShots (now owned by Kodak) became available, I transitioned to it and let the lab scan all my images. That represented a major improvement in my workflow, saving both time and money.

Having all images available digitally is extremely beneficial for my studio. By having the images scanned and put into the computer I can create ProShots web albums (a web site with all the images for each event) for each of my clients, work with them in Montage (album planning software) to create albums, or drag the images into Photoshop and show the clients the effects of cropping, conversion to black & white, and different creative techniques we can use on their images. The clients love being able to see all the possibilities, and if you show it to them they will buy it. Working with my image presentation this way has allowed customers to explore alternatives and has dramatically increased my sales. A side benefit is that they enjoy the process a lot more.

Working with a digital presentation system has also decreased costs, since we now do all our ordering work on the computer. We no longer have to sort or card negatives, and keeping track of the orders has become easier.

Adding My First Digital Camera. Over time I kept adding more and more digital techniques and tools to my business. Eventually I came to believe that if I did not purchase a digital camera I would get so far behind in learning the technology that I would never catch up. I finally took the plunge while on a trip to New York. I purchased the Olympus C-3030 camera. What a blast! It was so exciting to see the images right away! Although we typically don't consider using "amateur"/point-and-shoot cameras in this business, this little camera really packs a punch! I've won an award with an image that I took with this camera. Recognizing the potential, I quite quickly upgraded to bigger and better cameras—but we still have the Olympus and I still love it. We use it for most of our personal photography. It is sharp and easy to use, and does really well with exposure control.

Images by Penny Adams.

Image by Penny Adams.

I currently use the Canon 1D and the Canon D30. Canon was an easy choice because I already had quite a collection of Canon lenses and equipment. In addition to reducing the investment costs, I can still use my film-based cameras as backups to the digitals. I started with the D30, and while the long battery life was a big plus, I found it lacking in other areas. The autofocus system was very weak; I could never rely on it to perform well, and it was extremely slow, especially in low light situations. The autoexposure proved to be unreliable, as well. It was very frustrating to work with at weddings, yet the overall results were fantastic! The D30 was an early offering by Canon, and the issues we faced were typical of those experienced by early-adapters.

When I purchased the 1D, I found that Canon had indeed improved their technology, addressing most of the issues I encountered with the D30. The 1D is much more reliable and accurate in the focusing and exposure control. The image quality is excellent—my clients can't tell the difference between the digital image and a film image. In many cases, they actually prefer the digital capture because the colors tend to be truer and the images have more pop. Although it is much heavier than the D30, it is still easy to handle. The 1D also has better resolution at higher ISO settings. At the 800 setting there are some artifacts, but they just look like film grain, rather than pixels. We typically work at 400 ISO. We've experimented with different ISO settings, and I don't recommend going any higher than 800. The one aspect that I am not as happy with is the battery. It is the main reason the camera is heavier, and it does not last nearly as long as the D30's battery, although it is rechargeable. Unfortunately, battery technology seems to lag behind the rest of the electronics industry, so this is something that we'll have to put up with for the next few years.

With both cameras, the only flash that Canon recommends is the 550ex. Canon did not consider double lighting with studio strobes when they developed this flash, and early on we experienced some real problems when using the flash at receptions where we would set up extra studio lights on the dance floor. Canon reps have, so far, not been able to give me an accurate answer on how to solve this problem, so we generally shoot with the flash on manual and adjust our exposure compensation, since this can vary depending on the angle of the camera to the additional strobes.

Many photographers express concern about the difference in the effective focal length in digital cameras, but this has not really bothered me. I use the viewfinder and compose what I see.

Opportunities and Experimentation. Having a digital camera really opened up all sorts of opportunities for me. The best part of using digital cameras is that they have made me a better photographer. Now when I take a picture I can see if there is something wrong with the image—whether it is the exposure, the cropping, or the composition. Because I see the problem immediately, not only can I fix it and take another picture, but I also recognize the cause and learn how to avoid it in the future.

Because there is no added cost to taking pictures with the digital camera, I am taking more time to experiment with various techniques and equipment. I recently instituted a weekly assignment program for all of us at the studio. Every Friday we have a new challenge put in front of us, each designed to make us think in innovative ways, and for the next week we use the digital cameras and work on our assignments. One assignment was creating images that fit the title *Sounds of Silence*. Another assignment was to photograph themes, like

"texture," "weight," or "news." Yet another was to photograph the same scene with different focal lengths. The creativity level has skyrocketed! We have been using filters we never used before, we've used lenses in different ways than we normally thought of, finding photographic possibilities in scenes we would normally have ignored. Previously we might have considered trying some of these, but we would have drastically reduced the number of different techniques we'd try due to the film and printing costs. Digital photography encourages us to experiment and to explore our creativity, which results in allowing us to offer more to our clients.

Images by Penny Adams.

There are many benefits of incorporating digital technology into your studio; this was just one example. Other benefits are the reduced cost in film and proofing, quicker turnaround for some prints, and creative opportunities.

Challenges of Digital Photography. Digital photography is not without its headaches. I consider myself "technically challenged," so, for me, the learning

Images by Penny Adams.

curve is pretty steep. Making sure that we have only one copy of a session or portrait, and that it is the latest version, proved to be a major issue. We've instituted procedures to eliminate the problem, but the simple fact that an image can reside on multiple computers means the potential for this to recur exists.

Getting your images printed properly is also challenging, since both you and the lab are struggling to find the right way to do it. The labs are still shaking the kinks out of their digital processes (their digital workflow), and we are working with them to find the best way to preprocess the images to maximize their effectiveness and reduce the amount of reprinting. If you decide to print your own images, then you have to add in the entire workload associated with doing this—as well as the added cost of the equipment, materials, and maintenance.

Another factor is learning to control your exposures, which is much more critical with digital capture. The latitude in negative film made it almost too easy for us in the past! I have definitely become more critical of my exposures and have learned to use exposure compensation.

With digital cameras, the cost of ownership has dramatically increased. It used to be that the life expectancy of a camera was at least seven to ten years, more for the higher-end medium format cameras. There were improvements in cameras, but quantum leaps were uncommon. Therefore, while I still use my twenty-year-old Hasselblad every week, the life expectancy of my digital cameras is more like three years. As recently as 2000, an affordable digital camera had a resolution of only 2 megapixels. Today we can't consider anything under 3 megapixels, and 6-megapixel models are becoming the norm. Canon recently released an 11 megapixel camera, pushing the limits even higher. New advances in technology, such as the Foveon X3, sensors are threatening to usher in a whole new generation of low-cost cameras that will allow large-size prints.

Another issue is the infrastructure cost to support digital. Almost all of our work is done on computers these days, so in my studio I've been adding a new computer every year. The older ones are at the end of their effective lifespan and now have to be replaced or at least need major upgrades to the operating system, memory, and disks—all of which drives up the ongoing costs. The networking infrastructure required in a hybrid Macintosh/PC environment also introduces challenges, both technical and operational.

Image by Penny Adams.

The general availability of good quality digital cameras that anyone can buy and use is also an issue. Coupled with a population that is becoming more computer literate and has access to easy-to-use programs and hardware, this will result in fewer prints purchased from professional photographers for events. Another major factor is the quality of low-cost scanners. This allows customers to easily make high-resolution copies of photographs, and while this is clearly a copyright violation, it won't be enforceable. This will cut into the sales of multiple prints. Customers are now requesting CDs of all their photos, and expect this at a nominal cost. With the quality of printers available in the $80 to $200 range (and which most people already own), this would eliminate many orders. Even images stored at lower resolution can be improved using common software, at least to the point where they would be acceptable to many viewers.

There are solutions to the above, but none are simple. Technology today is geared toward the much larger consumer market, not professionals, so we can only expect that this situation will get worse with time. The only real answer is that professional wedding and portrait photographers need to change their business model, making it more in line with that of commercial photographers who primarily charge for services. There are many implications to this, and the only sure result is that the management of our business will change—*significantly*.

Filmless Society. Digital photography has certainly changed the face of photography, and the future is going to be an interesting one. People speculate on the possibility of a filmless society. I think the answer is a definite yes, and many mainstream photographers are either there or are well on their way. There will always be the diehards who will continue to print their own images, but it will become a novelty or specialty processing, much like using plate glass–based cameras are now. From the general consumer perspective, the transition is going to be even faster. A friend of mine recently marveled that her one-year-old daughter will never hold a film camera in her hands and will never know what film capture was like.

Final Thoughts. In summary, I would say that the digital experience has been tremendous. It has opened new doors for us and allowed us to become more creative, offer more to our clients, and increase our sales. The bottom line is that I became a photographer because I enjoyed the creative aspect of the job. Digital photography has enabled me to continue this. The reduction of costs that this has introduced has also allowed me to experiment more, and to rediscover my love for photography.

2

DIGITAL CAMERAS

After a photographer is comfortable with their first digital camera and has at least a working knowledge of the other aspects involved in digital imaging, it is then time to invest in a professional digital camera. This decision should be made carefully and after the photographer has evaluated their unique situation and their desired end result. The key is matching equipment with the type of photography you do the most and the type of product that you deliver to the client.

For a portrait photographer who primarily photographs large family groups and sells their clients 30x40-inch (and larger) prints, a digital camera or digital camera back for a medium format camera that has extremely large file sizes would fit the bill. The Canon 1DS, Kodak 14N, and digital backs made by Leaf, Phase One, Megavision, and others would be the right choice.

For the portrait photographer who photographs high school seniors, children, engagement sessions, and general portraits, any of the popular 35mm digital cameras will be sufficient. Most photographers choose a 35mm digital model based on the 35mm film cameras and lenses that they already own. This makes the most sense, since the lenses are interchangeable and there is no need to buy new ones. For example, Canon cameras (and a couple of the first Kodak digitals) have Canon lens mounts. Since numerous photographers already have Canon film cameras, it is only logical for them to choose one of the Canon digital cameras. If the photographer already owned Nikon 35mm film cameras, then he would choose one of the Nikon, Fuji, or newer Kodak models that use Nikon lens mounts. All of the professional digital cameras do a very good job and are more than adequate to fulfill the portrait photographer's needs.

Many photographers choose to integrate digital photography by using their digital cameras for business portraits or other "quick" sessions. For these sessions that only need a small-size image for output, one of the consumer or prosumer digital cameras will be sufficient. For this purpose, many photographers are using the better low-end cameras from Nikon, Canon, Fuji, Kodak, and Olympus.

All of the professional digital cameras do a very good job and are more than adequate.

◻ GENERAL CAMERA FEATURES

Today, there are literally dozens of professional digital cameras for the photographer to choose from. Where do you begin in making a selection? The easiest way to make an informed decision is to identify the features that are most important to you and the type of photography for which you will use your digital camera.

File Size. It is important to remember that one single digital camera may not fulfill all of your photography needs. For example, if you shoot a number of large family groups and routinely sell 20x24-inch, 30x40-inch, or 40x60-inch images to your clients, you will need a digital camera with a very large file size—preferably 12 megapixels or higher. A couple of the high-end 35mm digital cameras and all of the medium format digital backs would fill this need nicely.

ISO. The same cameras may not be the best choice for photographing a high school football or basketball game. For these types of events, file size is less important because the maximum size you will probably be expected to provide is 8x10 inches. Speed is of far greater importance in these cases. Many of the 35mm digital cameras have variable ISO speed selections from 100–3200 ISO. This ISO range will allow you to capture digital images in almost any lighting situation. Just like with film, the higher the selected ISO, the more grain or digital noise will be apparent in the image. Both Canon and Nikon have created 35mm cameras specifically designed for this purpose. The cameras have very high burst rates, meaning that they can capture several frames per second for a few seconds before the camera needs to stop and render all of the images. These are ideal for sporting events and some wedding photographers who enjoy shooting several frame sequences in order to capture that perfect moment for the bride and groom.

Image by Patrick Rice.

Shutter Delay. For the most part, camera manufacturers have solved the problems that plagued earlier digital cameras. Shutter delay—the time between when you press the shutter button and when the camera actually records the image—is no longer a problem with professional digital cameras. The older Nikon 950 and 990 cameras that we use for infrared imaging have some shutter delay, but we have learned through experience to be aware of this problem when taking pictures.

Flash Units. In many photographic situations, there will not be enough ambient light to record the image in the desired way. In these situations, the photographer will need a portable flash unit or studio lights to properly illuminate their subject. Both Canon and Nikon have introduced specific flash units designed to be used with their digital cameras. These dedicated portable strobes optimize all of the camera's features and allow for total integration of features and performance. For example, when using Canon digital cameras with their 550ex flashes, the camera can have flash synchronization from 30 seconds up to $\frac{1}{4000}$ of a second. If you use a non-Canon flash, the flash synchronization will be from 30 seconds to only $\frac{1}{250}$ of a second.

Image by Patrick Rice.

Photographers can certainly still use their non-manufacturer strobe units (i.e. Metz, Quantum, Lumedyne, Vivitar, etc.) with their digital cameras. However, there is a remote possibility that you can short out your digital camera when doing so. Strobe units that are matched to the camera send a regulated amount of voltage into the camera through the camera's hot shoe. Non-manufacturer strobe units may produce variable amounts of voltage and burn up the electronics in the camera. This type of malfunction is specifically not covered under any camera's warranty. To avoid this type of problem, we use a product called a safe sync. The safe sync, made by Wein and other companies, regulates the voltage from the portable flash unit to a consistent 6 volts. These units cost about $60 and fit right on top of the hot shoe mount on the camera and have a PC cord plug on them. The unit acts in much the same way a surge protector does for your desktop computer, protecting the camera from power surges from flash units. We see it as cheap insurance, and we have safe syncs on every digital camera we use. The same is true for studio lighting units. We use ProPhoto lights in our studio and have for many years. We simply plug the ProPhoto lights into the safe sync and shoot like we did with our film cameras.

CCD vs. CMOS. Another digital camera consideration is CCD vs. CMOS sensors. Most consumer digital cameras and some professional digital cameras use a Charge Coupled Device (or CCD) sensor. CCD sensors employ an array of photodiodes arranged in a grid pattern. Used as imaging devices since the 1970s, the first CCDs produced tiny images that were only 320x240 pixels—but pixel density has steadily increased over the years, and we now see 6-megapixel (3000x2000 pixels) sensors in some of the high-end digital cameras from Nikon,

Fuji, and Kodak. All CCD-based cameras use interpolation to create images, turning smaller amounts of data into larger files by using the camera's on-board processor to generate additional data based on neighboring pixels.

Canon was the first professional digital camera to use a CMOS imaging sensor instead of a CCD. CMOS (Complementary Metal Oxide Semiconductor) sensors have some advantages over CCD-type sensors. They use only a fraction (10 to 20 percent) of the power that CCDs do, making them attractive for battery-powered cameras. CMOS sensors are made using the same circuitry technology as CPUs and RAM memory, so they also cost less to produce than CCDs, which require specialized fabrication equipment.

Like CCDs, CMOS sensors use an array of photodiodes to convert light into electronic signals. The major difference between CCDs and CMOS sensors is in the way the stored charges, which are quite weak, are enhanced and converted into a usable signal.

A CCD sensor scans its pixels consecutively, shifting stored charges from each row down to the next row and toward the bottom of the array, then outputting the charges in the final row in a serial stream. The voltage levels of each pixel in the serial stream are increased by an on-chip amplifier prior to output, and sent to either an external or internal analog-to-digital converter (ADC) where the signals are converted into the array of bytes that makes up the image.

Image by Patrick Rice.

In contrast, each pixel in a CMOS sensor has its *own* amplifier circuit, so the signal amplification is performed prior to the image being scanned. The resulting signal is strong enough to be used without any further processing. Unlike CCDs, CMOS sensors often contain additional image processing circuitry (including analog-to-digital converters and JPEG compression processors) directly on the chip, making it easier and faster to retrieve and process the picture information. This results in increased reliability, reduced power consumption, and a more compact design.

Until the introduction of the first Canon CMOS professional camera, the Canon D30, CMOS sensors were generally regarded as a low-cost, low-quality alterative to CCD sensors and were typically found in inexpensive digital cameras. A major problem in older CMOS sensors was that pixels often had more or less sensitivity than their neighboring pixels. This unevenness translates into noise. Canon solved the noise problem in the D30 by scanning the sensor twice, once before the shutter opens and again while the shutter is open. The "dark" (closed-shutter) image is electronically subtracted from the exposed image, which virtually eliminates the noise.

So what does all of this mean to the professional photographer trying to choose a chip platform?

So what does all of this mean to the professional photographer trying to choose a chip platform? With the innovations of the past couple of years, it doesn't make that much difference whether your camera uses a CCD or CMOS sensor. Canon, Nikon, Fuji, and Kodak are all producing great digital cameras that produce outstanding files for the working professional photographer. While there are differences in the two technologies, I do not feel that the sensor is necessarily the deciding factor when choosing a camera. My recommendation to any photographer is quite simple: If you already own 35mm camera lenses on the Canon platform, then choose one of the Canon digital cameras. If, however, you own 35mm lenses on the Nikon platform, then choose the Nikon, Fuji, or Kodak digital camera bodies. The key is to not have to reinvest in new lenses. This will save you thousands of dollars and you will get great digital files regardless of which sensor your camera utilizes.

☐ A PROFESSIONAL PERSPECTIVE

Custom White Balance: The Start of Something Great, by Michael Ayers
My camera of choice is Fujifilm's S-2 Pro. It's lightweight, fast, user-friendly, accurate, priced to sell, and gives me spectacular skin tones. Why such great color? Fujifilm claims it is because they are a company that creates color—start to finish, from capture to final prints. At any rate, one of the S-2 Pro's unique features is the ability to set up two custom white balance settings and save them within the camera's memory. This digital tool saves time later because every subsequent image captured in similar lighting conditions is perfectly color balanced and needs no correction in Adobe Photoshop. In a busy studio, this powerful tool can save two to ten hours of computer labor per week! I always place my studio's white-balance characteristics into one of the camera's memory spots and leave the other white balance memory for whatever lighting condition I'm working with at the time. I regularly use Tamron's 28–70mm f/2.8 zoom lens because it lets me zoom right

Image by Michael Ayers.

into a small white-balance card that I keep stuck with Velcro on the back of my flash. Practice saving your custom white-balance settings quickly, so it becomes second nature!

◼ DIGITAL STORAGE MEDIA

With today's professional digital cameras, the photographer has a few choices with regard to storage media for their images. The most popular are microdrives, CompactFlash (CF) cards, and Smart Media cards. Most cameras can accommodate microdrives and either CF or Smart Media cards, but usually not both.

Microdrives came on the market very early in the evolution of digital imaging, offering large storage capacity and fast read and write speeds in the camera and computer. They were also very inexpensive compared to CompactFlash and Smart Media cards. The major disadvantage of microdrives is that they are miniature computer hard drives that have moving parts enclosed in the housing.

Image by Barbara Rice.

This presents two distinct problems. First, if a microdrive is dropped, it is possible that it may never work again, and the photographer could lose every image on the microdrive at the time. This has happened to a number of photographers. The second problem is that a microdrive can crash just like any other computer hard drive. I haven't met a photographer who has not had their computer crash at one time or another, making it necessary to replace their hard drive and reinstall everything that was on the computer before it crashed. These potential disasters mean that using microdrives presents a considerable risk for the professional portrait or wedding photographer.

We have chosen to use CompactFlash cards with our Canon and Nikon digital cameras. These cards are solid-state circuits with no moving parts to break. The cards are practically indestructible! I have met three photographers who have left CompactFlash cards in the pockets of their trousers and sent them through the washing machine and dryer without harming the card or the images recorded on them. CompactFlash cards were initially very expensive, had limited storage capacity, and very slow read and write speeds. This has all changed. The prices of CompactFlash cards have dropped dramatically—so much so that the 1GB are nearly as inexpensive as microdrives of the same storage size. Storage capacity for CompactFlash cards has actually surpassed that which is available for microdrives. Lexar Media has introduced 1GB, 2GB and 4GB Compact-Flash cards for professional image-makers. These large-capacity cards can store hundreds of files and accommodate the latest 12- and 14-megapixel cameras. Last, the read and write speeds of professional CompactFlash cards have also surpassed that of microdrives, with Lexar Media introducing 40x speed CompactFlash cards.

◻ IMAGE RECOVERY SOFTWARE

Image recovery has become a major concern for today's digital photographer. Many companies now offer image recovery software to locate files on cards that are unreadable, images that have accidentally been deleted, and other worst-case scenarios for the photographer. Lexar Media guarantees their professional cards for life and provides free card replacement and image recovery at their factory. Moreover, they have provided many camera stores with the same recovery software so the photographer can take their problem CompactFlash card to a local lab when image recovery is required. Not only that, but now Lexar Media has included the image recovery software in the card itself and provides a free USB port and jump-shot cable with their professional cards. This extensive customer support has made us very loyal supporters of Lexar Media CompactFlash cards.

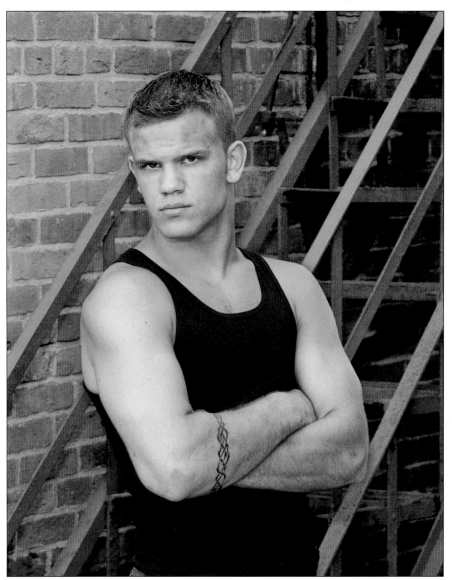

Image by Mark Bohland.

◻ A PROFESSIONAL PERSPECTIVE

Shooting Square with the Canon 10D, by Mark Bohland

I've photographed weddings since the early 1980s using square-format cameras ranging from a Mamiya C330 twin-lens outfit to a Bronica SqA. Shooting square has so many advantages at weddings that it just made sense to continue using that format with my new digital camera. Among other things, shooting square allows me to:

• See the entire train of a bride's dress and still be as close to her as if I had shot vertically and cut off the train of her dress
• Shoot closer full-length images of a large wedding party without the wasted space on the left and right of a horizontal rectangular print

- Work quickly without having to rotate my camera and/or flash to accommodate vertical or horizontal situations

I took a Canon 10D to a wedding I photographed with a Bronica to do a few test shots. My favorite images from the wedding were from the 10D, and I've photographed every wedding since digitally. However, the original file shot with the 10D at its highest resolution is 3072x2048 pixels. That translates into an 8x12-inch image at 256 pixels per inch. It's immediately apparent that even photographers who want to print rectangular 8x10-inch prints (or any other 1:1.25-proportioned prints) are going to have to crop part of the 10D file. Cropping is a given; but how much can be cropped without sacrificing quality, and how can we know exactly what will be cropped while we're looking through the 10D viewfinder?

My lab can make an exceptional 20x30-inch print from the full 3072x2048-pixel 10D file. A cropped 2560x2048-pixel file yields a 20x24-inch print, a 2048x2048-pixel file yields a 20x20-inch print, and a 1638x2048-pixel file yields a 16x20-inch print. The constant in all of these files is the 2048 pixel dimension, which is roughly represented by the entire image from top to bottom in the 10D viewfinder, when the camera is held horizontally. But how can we determine how much of the left-to-right image in the viewfinder represents 2048 pixels?

Fortunately, Canon has given us cropping guides right in the viewfinder, in the form of its five horizontal focusing points. The area from the left edge of the left focusing point to the right edge of the right focusing point roughly represents 2048 pixels. As long as we keep our subject within the top and bottom of the viewfinder and between the farthest left and right focusing points, we can crop the desired image to a square format in Photoshop.

When working with digital image files, it is essential to establish a routine to ensure that files are handled safely and consistently. After downloading files from the camera to a folder on my computer's hard drive, I make a copy of that fold-

Images by Mark Bohland.

Image by Mark Bohland.

er and its files, and as an added precaution I burn a CD of that same folder and files. I never open the original files. That way if I need to, I can always go back and start over again by copying a previously unopened file.

To crop the 10D files to 2048x2048 pixel files in Photoshop, I select the cropping tool and use the options palette to set a fixed target size of 8x8 inches with a resolution of 256 pixels per inch (8 x 256 = 2048). I drag the cropping tool across the entire image from top to bottom, making sure to start and finish outside the image. This ensures that I am selecting all of the pixels from the top to the bottom of the image. I then adjust the selection from left to right to choose the area I want to crop, and finally press Enter to crop the image.

The Canon 10D can easily provide all the advantages of digital imaging without sacrificing the benefits of shooting in a square format.

3

DIGITAL PORTRAIT PHOTOGRAPHY

Portrait photography has long been regarded as one of the truest expressions of a photographer's artistic ability. The rendering of a subject's mood, feelings, and even their soul, is one of the most gratifying aspects of portraiture. The world of digital photography has made it easier for photographic artists to capture the essence of their subjects through its speed, ease of use, and instant feedback.

■ ASSURED SUCCESS

How many times have photographers thought they had a great portrait image, only to be disappointed days later after they received their prints back from the lab? This is not the case with digital. Every image can be viewed instantly only seconds after it was recorded. Most digital cameras have the ability to zoom in on the image, allowing photographers to study detail and check sharpness. A review of the image's histogram will illustrate the tonal range of the exposure and reveal any areas that are over- or underexposed and therefore unprintable. Not since the invention of the Polaroid back for medium format cameras has the photographer had the ability to view the images at the time of the photo session. Digital, however, is more accurate than Polaroid film,

Image by Barbara Rice.

since you are actually viewing the *exact image* that the camera recorded and not a similar image with a different film source that may not have the same characteristics of the film in the camera back.

With digital photography, we can also take more images than we would with film. Since we do not proof our portrait images (see below), we have no costs involved other than our time. Our clients feel they are getting more for their money since we are not limited to the typical twelve to fifteen exposures that we would have made with film capture.

Image by Barbara Rice.

Clients also react very positively to digital portrait photography because they know exactly what the images will look like before they receive their prints. Changes and modifications in clothing, makeup, and hairstyle are easily made at the time of the portrait session to ensure that every client is happy with their portrait images. We gladly show our clients some of the images during the session to both create confidence in our abilities as artists and to make sure they like themselves and the poses we chose. It is impossible for a client to dislike a photograph if they had input in its creation and approved it during the session. There are no surprises when the finished photos are delivered.

◼ EASY IMAGE SELECTION

Before any studio portrait session, the client is informed that they will view and select their portraits only minutes after the portrait session is complete. We allow about half an hour for the clients to make their choices. We use Fuji's StudioMaster PRO workflow software, which allows us to quickly group the images for comparison. We have the client narrow down the images to their favorites in groups of four images at a time. Once we have their favorite images selected, we then determine the quantities and sizes. It's just that easy.

Not producing proofs forces the clients to make their decisions at the time of the setting, right after they view the images for the first time. Clients are always most excited immediately after a session. As time passes, this excitement wanes. By getting the client to order immediately, our sales are higher than they were when the client had to return to the studio to view the proofs.

Not having paper proofs has also cut down on the illegal copying of our images. Again, digital portrait photography has resulted in higher sales because our images are not being reproduced at the local copy shop.

◼ VERSATILITY

Another advantage of digital portrait photography is the ability to seamlessly create black & white and sepia photographs for the clients. With film, we needed to

Image by Barbara Rice.

change film or camera backs to provide the client with both color images and black & white images. This meant more time on the session and more cost to both the studio and the client. Invariably, some client would ask if a particular image that was recorded on black & white film could be made in color. The clients were always somewhat disappointed when told that was not possible.

Using imaging software like Photoshop, converting a digital color image to black & white is fast, easy, and accurate. Images maintain their contrast and range with no loss of quality. Creating sepia-toned photographs is just as easy. Photoshop now contains a built-in sepia toning action in the actions palette, so all you need to do it hit play and it's done. There is no additional software to buy, and you can adjust the intensity and tone of the sepia effect you are looking for. Selective coloring or spot coloring is also a snap with digital. Using Photoshop tools such as layer masking, you can easily turn an image black & white and then reveal the original color that is hidden underneath the black & white layer.

Converting a digital color image to black & white is fast, easy, and accurate.

◼ CLOTHING CONSIDERATIONS

Clothing considerations for digital portraiture are not that different than with film capture. With all of our portrait clients, we send out a brochure that clearly explains how to dress for the portrait session. It illustrates the right and wrong way to coordinate outfits with images. This has greatly helped in communicating to the clients what to wear for their session. Patterns and stripes have always been discouraged because they are distracting in the photograph. In our studio portraiture, we tend to not have extremely high-contrast lighting ratios; this helps to avoid the problem of blown-out whites and no-detail blacks.

◼ LIGHTING

Lighting considerations for digital photography are not all that much different than they are for film photography with one big exception: the photographer has more lighting control with digital cameras.

White Balance. The three primary colors (red, green, and blue) exist in all lighting situations at varying degrees. When the color temperature of a scene is low, then there is more red, but when the color temperature is high, there is more blue. As the color temperature changes from low to high, the color cast changes accordingly. As an example, a subject lit in tungsten light will look more red or orange, and a subject lit in fluorescent light will look more green.

The human eye is very adaptive and quickly compensates for different lighting conditions so that colors appear natural regardless of the lighting situation (color temperature). Cameras are not so adaptive. Cameras record the color temperature that exists. With film cameras, a photographer had to choose the proper film to match the color temperature of the light that the photo would be taken under; otherwise he would get a color cast. For example, daylight-balanced film would give an orangish color to wedding photographs taken in a typical church that is illuminated by incandescent light bulbs (tungsten light)—especially with longer exposures. The photographer could also place a color correction filter in front of the camera lens to adjust the film to the light.

With digital cameras, this is no longer necessary. All professional digital cameras give the photographer a selection of lighting options for matching the camera to the shooting situation. These options are commonly referred to as white-balance (WB) settings. The digital photographer can change the white-balance setting on his camera at any time to match the lighting conditions present. Most cameras also have an auto white-balance (AWB) setting that can be used as the default setting for any lighting situation. In the AWB mode, the camera's sensor automatically chooses the best white-balance setting for the lighting that it

Image by Penny Adams.

detects. This is a huge time saver for the wedding photographer, who has to work quickly and doesn't have time to change film types or place filters in front of each lens.

Digital cameras have several preset white-balance options to match any lighting situation. Besides the auto white-balance setting, the photographer can set the camera more specifically by choosing one of the specific white-balance settings—usually depicted in symbols. The symbol of the sun is for bright, sunny days. The symbol showing clouds is for cloudy, hazy, or overcast days. The symbol depicting a lightbulb is for tungsten light. The symbol depicting a fluorescent bulb is for fluorescent light. The symbol showing a lightning bolt is for flash photography. Some cameras show a symbol that depicts shade for subjects placed in shaded areas of the scene. Most digital cameras have a custom white-balance setting where the photographer can shoot a white card and use that data as the standard for the white setting in that scene. More advanced digital cameras have a Kelvin-degree setting where the photographer can manually set the exact color temperature for a particular scene using a color temperature meter.

Flash Photography. For flash photography, the photographer has several options. The first is to use a flash specifically designed by the camera manufacturer to work directly with the digital camera brand. With the Canon flash units that we use, the flash can sync at shutter speeds from 30 seconds to $1/4000$ of a second. This is ideal for fill flash situations outdoors when you need a little light in the subject's eyes but you do not want to overpower the natural light with the strobe. In addition, full through-the-lens (TTL) metering capabilities exist with these dedicated flash units so that the photographer can allow the computer in the camera to determine how much light is necessary for proper exposures in almost any situation.

Digital cameras have several preset white-balance choices to match any lighting situation.

Photographers can still use other flash equipment with their digital cameras. Most every digital camera has a PC connection and a hot shoe on the camera body. Using these, your flash can be plugged into your digital camera in the same way that you plugged it into your old film cameras. We plug our PC cord into the safe sync on the digital camera and use our ProPhoto lighting for all of our studio portraits.

For all of our flash photography, we find that, of all the white balance choices, the flash-mode selection (lightning bolt icon) gives the most pleasing skin tones in our images. The images in the flash mode are a little warmer than those in the auto white balance mode.

Image by Patrick Rice.

WINDOW LIGHTING

Window light portraiture has always been attractive. It is the same for digital. This type of lighting has the ability to produce beautifully soft images. Just as when we are illuminating a subject with lights, we look for window-light situations that offer softer light contrast. If the light entering the window is too harsh, we simply balance it with a reflector to pop in light on the shadow side. There are, of course, times when we want high-contrast portraits. This is especially true with high-school senior boys, where the use of high contrast and an intentional lack of detail adds to the mood of the overall image. However, for most subjects, a low- to medium-contrast lighting pattern is the most pleasing.

DIGITAL METERING AND EXPOSURE

The question comes up quite often "How do you meter for digital?" My answer is that you meter for digital the same way you metered for slide film. With any exposure, film or digital, it is best to be accurate.

If you are using a handheld meter, you simply take a reading of the light from the subject back to camera position. The measuring instrument of the meter (usually a dome) should be facing the main light source in a studio situation. This method will always give an accurate reading.

If you are using your camera's built-in meter, you will get a reflected meter reading off the subject. In other words, what you target with the camera's built-in meter will determine your exposure in any of the camera's program or automatic modes. When a camera meter targets a white area of the subject, it will determine that you need less exposure than if it targets a black area of the subject. The better the digital camera, the more advanced the built-in metering system—usually measured in how many "points" or areas of the scene it targets to properly average an accurate reading. The latest generation of professional 35mm digital cameras have greatly improved the camera's built-in metering systems.

Image by Michael Ayers.

A great advantage of digital photography over film is that the photographer can quickly check the exposure by reviewing the histogram of the image. The histogram shows the dynamic range of each image from black to white. With most digital cameras, overexposed areas will "blink" on the histogram to tell the photographer there is no detail in those particular highlight areas. This feature is invaluable to all photographers. We constantly review our histograms on every photo assignment and make adjustments as necessary. This kind of exposure control was impossible or impractical until the digital age.

◻ A PROFESSIONAL PERSPECTIVE

Histograms: Why Use a Light Meter?, by Michael Ayers

At a recent photography seminar, a student asked me how much I use my light meter. I then asked, "What's a light meter?" The point is this: why use a light meter under general circumstances when you can display histograms for each image on the LCD panel on the back of the camera body? The reason this power tool is so useful is that I can immediately check the exact exposure information for any captured image. Photographers who are not good at reading histograms within Adobe Photoshop or on the back of their cameras, should try to make this special talent second nature! All image-makers in the new millennium must be familiar with Levels in Photoshop and how to fully adjust an image in all three RGB channels, including lightening, darkening, and saturation in both input and output. The levels of the histograms on the back of the camera simply allow photographers to preview what can be seen in Photoshop later. Therefore, if an image is over- or underexposed, having this information just after the shutter is released is critical. This data is impossible to acquire with a film camera, and it can save a dozen hours a week in image adjustment time.

Getting Portrait Clients Excited about Digital, by Chad Tsoufiou

Many high schoolers do not like having their picture taken—this is especially true of the boys. Recently, I was doing a senior portrait session for a young man who didn't care what outfits he was going to wear or even if he had his picture taken at all. He was only cooperative because his mom wanted the pictures taken. Shooting digitally, I was able to show him the portraits I was creating several times during the session. Eventually, this instant feedback got him involved—he even started telling me what he wanted.

Because of this, I was able to give him and his mom exactly what they wanted—and then I gave them even more. With the boy posed leaning against a fence, I got out my Nikon Coolpix camera and shot a digital color infrared picture. After I showed him the image, the senior who two hours before didn't even

Image by Chad Tsoufiou.

want his pictures taken was suddenly excited about his photos. He even started asking me if I could take more. How's that for a testimony? It really goes to show how shooting digitally can provide great peace of mind for your subjects. In addition to keeping them entertained during the session, being able to instantly preview the images gives the client a chance to tell you what they like and what they don't. Because you can take as many shots as you want, refining as you go, you can finish a session knowing that both the client and the photographer are satisfied.

Of course, the advantages are not just for the clients. I've found that going digital has changed the way I take images. I no longer wonder how they are going to look when they come back from the lab—which means I don't have to worry about finding out that a flash wasn't firing, for example. Without wasting a frame of film or one Polaroid image, I can modify the pose, refine the lighting, or adjust the exposure on the spot. For images that need a little refinement, working digitally lets me make any needed adjustments to perfect the brightness and contrast and to do my own retouching without having to pay the lab. As a result, shooting digital means that when I send images to the lab, I already know they are all good—a very reassuring feeling.

■ HIGH-SCHOOL SPORTS PHOTOGRAPHY

Many photographers across the country have exclusive contracts with high schools in their area. These contracts allow the studio the opportunity to photograph every high-school senior for the yearbook and hopefully sell each student

Images by Robert Williams.

a photo package. One of the concessions most studios make to secure this contract is a promise to photograph school sporting events for inclusion in the yearbook.

School photographers made the switch to 35mm cameras years back because of their ease of use, lens speed, and the availability of longer focal-length lenses. However, shooting several rolls of 35mm film and having them processed was a costly exercise—especially when the school yearbook staff only needed one or two good images.

With digital photography, the photographer can take as many images at each event as he or she likes and provide the school with a CD of the images for them to choose from. The only real cost is the photographer's time.

Another big advantage of using digital cameras for shooting high school sports is the lens magnification due to the sensor size. Most digital 35mm cameras have a magnification factor of 1.4–1.6. This means that your lenses are actually a longer focal length than they are marked. For example, a 200mm lens on

Image by Ken Holida.

a digital camera with a 1.5 magnification is effectively a 300mm lens. This added focal length is a great asset for sports photography.

The ability of digital cameras to shoot at very high ISO settings is another advantage. Lighting for sports is always tricky because the photographer has to maintain shutter speeds high enough to "freeze" the action. Shooting in the 800, 1600, or even 3200 ISO range can enable the photographer to record images that he couldn't get otherwise.

◻ A PROFESSIONAL PERSPECTIVE

"Old-Time Photography" and the Digital Age, by Ron Burgess

One niche market in photography that few people know about is antique and amusement photography. This specialty is practiced by studios and operations that costume their clientele and provide them with images of themselves, in various "time periods," with appropriate backgrounds and props. They may use permanent sets and backdrops or they may be mobile. Their images may be solely for amusement or they may be taken to look "period correct." The goal is to make the clients happy by fulfilling their fantasy.

In the early days, most of these entrepreneurs started by using a system started by Agfa but changed to a Polaroid system. As digital technology improved, it started to make its way into this market. A few vendors even made realistic looking view cameras with a digital camera inside! Using the digital process, the customer enjoys the instant gratification of being able to view multiple poses in color or black & white. This instant previewing also makes it easier to sell custom packages as well as custom mats or posters.

One old-time photographer does his photography with a twist. He specializes in Civil War–era images and photographs his clients at Civil War and living history reenactments, as well as at Native American powwows. Using a late-1800s 5x7-inch Burke and James view camera, he provides his clients with 4x5-inch sepia-toned images. He also offers larger images that are taken with a professional digital camera. After previewing their images, the clients order what they want. Their images are not provided immediately, since maintaining the period authenticity of the reenactment requires that no electricity be used. Therefore, after the event, the subjects' images are mailed to them—and they have the opportunity to purchase reproduction Victorian photograph frames.

There are other people and other methods, but this gives you a unique look at the growing role of digital photography in the old-time photography industry.

Image by Ron Burgess.

DIGITAL WEDDING PHOTOGRAPHY

Digital photography is the latest evolutionary change in the field of wedding photography, and it offers exciting possibilities for both the photographer and the client. It is not necessary to capture the images with a digital camera to take advantage of many of the possibilities digital provides. Many wedding photographers still use film capture and then scan in their negatives so that the images can be altered, enhanced, and manipulated in programs such as Adobe Photoshop. We choose to use digital capture for the following reasons.

Our brides and grooms are excited that we can show them their images as they are taken.

With digital capture on the wedding day, we get to see every image that we take on the LCD screen on the back of cameras. This is vital because it tells us that the digital camera is working properly, what the image will look like, and if the exposure is correct. With regard to exposure, we can quickly check the camera's histogram to determine if we have covered the full range of the subject and its surroundings, and we can also determine if there are any unprintable areas in the image. With many digital cameras, areas that have blownout highlights will blink when viewing the histogram. Upon seeing this, the photographer can then make the necessary adjustments to the exposure to get a better quality image capture.

Our brides and grooms are excited that we can now show them their images as they are taken on the LCD screen. We can check expressions, see if eyes are open or closed, and see if there are any distracting elements that should be avoided or corrected. Brides love the fact that they can preview their images. There is no longer the question about how the images will look when they see their proofs, because they already know they will look great.

Though the years, I've always found it mildly amusing that people would come up to me at the end of a wedding and tell me that I did a great job. How did they know? How could they be sure? What if I never loaded film in the camera? What if the camera was not working properly? With digital capture on the wedding day I am much more comfortable accepting that compliment, because the clients *do* know that I did a great job.

◻ ADVANTAGES

Technology continues to change all aspects of our lives. This is especially true in the field of photography. Although many photographers refuse to embrace digital imaging, it is the best choice for both the photographer and the bride and

Image by Michael Ayers.

groom on their wedding day. There are many advantages to digital photography, but the following points outline some of the most important ones.

Visual Confirmation. First, with digital cameras, the photographer can view the LCD screen on the back of his camera to receive visual confirmation of the quality of each image that he creates. With film cameras, the photographer never really knows what the images will look like until after the film has been processed and printed at the lab. With a film camera, you could be experiencing mechanical problems with the camera but never know it until it was too late. This exact experience has plagued photographers for decades! With digital cameras, a photographer instantly knows if there is a camera problem, mistake in exposure, etc. With digital, you will never take two bad pictures in a row. This is quite a relief for the bride and groom, who are entrusting a photographer to record memories of their special day.

Image Security. Second, digital photographers now have complete image security. With film cameras, the photographer has to send the exposed film to the lab. There is always a risk that either the carrier service or the lab could lose or damage the film. In such cases, the photographer could do everything right, and yet the bride and groom might not get any photographs.

With digital photography this is no longer the case. You record each image onto CompactFlash media storage cards. Once you return to your studio, you transfer the images from the cards onto CDs. These CDs should never leave the studio. You can then copy the images on the CD to a duplicate disc and send that disc to the lab for the making of the photographic prints. If the disc is lost or damaged in transit or at the lab, you can simply burn another copy and resend it. As a result, the bride and groom never again have to worry about anything happening to their priceless images.

Versatility. Digital photographers can capture every image in color, but are free to make any color image into a perfect black & white photograph with absolutely no loss in quality. This is not possible with film, where there was always some quality degradation when making a color image into black & white. In addition, sepia toning and color toning of digital images is much easier and less costly than with film images.

Cropping. Finally, there is much more flexibility in the cropping of digital images. With film, the photographer must use standard cropping sizes (known as masks or crop cards). These crop cards do not always provide the ideal cropping of an image. With digital images, cropping is much more flexible and can maximize the photographic quality of each wedding image.

☐ DIGITAL INFRARED WEDDING PHOTOGRAPHY

Digital imaging is quickly taking hold in all aspects of amateur and professional photography. Digital camera advances are being made constantly. In just a few short years, we have seen the prices go down, while the image quality has gone up. Studios are quickly making the digital transition in all areas of the business.   Image by Patrick Rice.

Image by Tony Zimcosky.

As a wedding photographer who likes to create unconventional images, I have always enjoyed the unusual in photography. Many years ago, this quest to be different led me to fisheye lenses. In recent years, I have rediscovered black & white photography as well as black & white infrared photography. Unfortunately, in the digital world, these "outside the box" techniques are not as readily available.

Nikon Coolpix 950. Through research and discussion, I discovered that I could still produce my unique style of wedding photography using one particular digital camera—the Nikon Coolpix 950. The camera has a 2.11 megapixel CCD with Nikon's 256-element matrix metering system. The camera can be used in programmed autoexposure, shutter-priority auto, aperture-priority auto, and manual exposure modes. The built-in zoom lens gives you "true" focal lengths from 38–115mm (35mm equivalent).

The Nikon Coolpix 950 also has several size and quality modes to choose from when using the camera. The Coolpix 950 and other digital cameras store images as JPEG (short for Joint Photographic Experts Group) files. The camera has three modes of JPEG file compression: basic, normal, and fine—ranging from most compression to least compression. The less compression, the better the image quality upon enlargement of the image. You can also shoot in the uncompressed "hi mode" in TIF format for the best quality possible. Your only drawback is that you cannot store as many images using the better quality modes on the camera. For this reason, I use large capacity Lexar Compact-Flash cards with this camera.

So, what is it about this camera that makes it special anyway? For starters, Nikon makes a screw-on fisheye adapter lens for this and the other models of their Coolpix line of cameras. This was important because I was able to achieve a "true" fisheye image on a digital capture system. Other digital cameras either do not have a fisheye lens as an option or have a multiplication factor of about 1.5 on the SLR lenses used with the camera. For example, with the Nikon D1, the standard fisheye lens for this system no longer has the true fisheye appearance in the images. By attaching the Nikon fisheye adapter lens to the Nikon Coolpix camera's zoom lens, you can get "true" focal lengths from 8–24mm (35mm format)!

The other unusual feature with the Nikon Coolpix 950—the one that got me excited about the camera—was this camera's ability to shoot true infrared images. Infrared light is the band of invisible light that exists just

Image by Travis Hill.

beyond the red rays. Although the eye cannot see infrared light, it can be recorded with photographic film and also digitally. Infrared images are often considered dream-like or ethereal in appearance. It is a very striking and distinctive type of imaging.

To understand why this camera can shoot into the infrared range and others cannot, you must first understand how digital cameras are made and how infrared images are recorded. With digital cameras, manufacturers are always working to get the "cleanest" image capture possible to give the photographer the best image file. As manufacturers learned more about image capture, they discovered that they could get a cleaner image by blocking infrared light from being recorded. Apparently, invisible infrared light contaminates the visible light being captured on the digital media and thus degrades the image quality.

The solution was to install an infrared cut-off filter to block the transmission of all infrared light to the camera. In technical terms, these are referred to as hot-mirror filters. As the name implies, these filters reflect heat and transmit visible light. The latest hot-mirror filters transmit over 85 percent of the wavelengths in the 400–700 nanometer range (the visible light spectrum) and reflect (block) over 90 percent of the wavelengths in the 700–1000 nanometer range (the near-infrared spectrum). This discovery was made *after* the release of the Nikon Coolpix 950 camera—so this particular camera does not have an effective hot mirror/infrared cutoff filter in place. The Nikon Coolpix 990, 880, and other models now all have the more efficient cutoff filter.

The other reason that the Nikon Coolpix 950 can record into the infrared range is the fact that the camera has both a color and a black & white mode for recording images. In the black & white mode, with the proper filtration, a photographer can digitally record infrared images.

Filtration. The key to infrared recording of images is to use an infrared pass filter to block some or all of the visible light from being recorded. With Kodak infrared film, I primarily use a number 25 red filter (basic red) in front of the lens and get very good results. Trees, grass, and other foliage are recorded as very light gray or white, and blue skies can be nearly black with this film and filter.

The Nikon Coolpix cameras have a 28mm threaded ring on the front of the camera's zoom lens. I purchased a 28–37mm step-up ring along with a 37–49mm step-up ring and then attached a 49mm number 25 red filter to it. While this was my filter of choice for infrared images on film, it achieved only adequate results shooting digitally. The images I was recording with the digital camera just did not have the same "snap" that I was accustomed to with Kodak

Image by Jacob Jakuszeit.

infrared film. The next logical step was to use a filter that blocked more of the visible spectrum and was more responsive in the infrared range.

Opaque filters block all of the light rays shorter than 700nm and only allow the infrared light to pass. In appearance, the filters look black and cannot be seen through. When I used a 49mm number 87 (opaque) glass filter on my step-up ring configuration, the results rivaled that of Kodak infrared film! This was exciting and has changed my entire outlook on infrared image recording. (*Note:* I recently purchased a square of number 87 Kodak Wratten filter material, cut a piece out, and inserted it into the lip of a 28mm UV filter. The Wratten material is flexible enough to stay in place without falling out. To my knowledge, there are no commercially available number 87 filters in a 28mm filter size, so this is a practical alternative to using the step-up ring configuration described above. This allows me to use all of the Nikon adapter lenses when recording digital infrared images—including the fish-eye lens, wide angle–lens, and tele-photo-lens attachments. The creative possibilities are limitless!)

Shooting. When shooting digital infrared, the flash setting on the camera should be disabled. I make my exposures using the auto matrix-metering mode, working with the camera on a tripod. Exposures are relatively slow using this filter with the Nikon Coolpix 950; they range from about $\frac{1}{15}$ to 2 seconds in the sunlight. In overcast conditions, the exposure times are even longer, which makes it

Image by Patrick Rice.

difficult to record in-focus images of people on account of subject movement. As with infrared film, I generally place my digital photography subjects in the sunlight to maximize the infrared effect in the image.

Because you cannot see through opaque filters, I compose my images using the camera's small viewfinder window and not the larger LCD display. The image in this viewfinder corresponds to the image being recorded, even changing as the lens zooms in and out for different focal lengths.

To make an exposure, I either press down on the shutter very gently so I do not create any camera movement or I use the self-timer mode on the camera. The Nikon Coolpix 950 has two different self-timer settings. Once the camera is set for self-timer, if you depress the shutter once, the image will be recorded after ten seconds. However, if you depress the shutter twice, you will record the image after only three seconds. I use the shorter duration of the self-timer mode so that my subjects do not have to rigidly hold a pose for ten seconds or longer.

You have heard the expression "necessity is the mother of invention." Apparently, the designers at CKCPower.com have heard this too, because they created a camera bracket for the Nikon Coolpix 950 digital camera that has incorporated a cable release mechanism. This means you no longer need to use the self-timer or attempt to depress the shutter without shaking the camera. The bracket threads onto the camera's tripod socket and it also has a –20 thread on the bottom of the bracket to thread onto a tripod. I attach a Bogen 3157 quick-release plate to the bottom of the bracket so that I can quickly attach this camera and bracket assembly to the Bogen 3265 head on my tripod. The bracket is designed to rotate out of the way without having to be disassembled for the changing of batteries or CompactFlash cards.

I have found there is still some camera shake—especially at longer exposures. So I approached the designers at Custom Brackets, Inc. about designing a more suitable camera bracket for the Nikon Coolpix cameras. This design is far more rigid and there is no camera shake at any shutter speed.

I have found there is still some camera shake—especially at longer exposures.

Modifying Cameras. Since I am always looking to perfect my imaging, I was very interested when I heard that some photographers were modifying their digital cameras for better infrared image recording. In a nutshell, photographers are removing the hot-mirror filter in the camera and replacing it with clear glass of the same size. It is important to replace the filter with glass or the camera will be "near-sighted" and not record images sharply.

I contacted my local camera repair shop (Pro Camera Inc. in Cleveland, OH) and asked them to consider modifying one of my Nikon Coolpix 950 cameras. Being a Nikon repair facility and familiar with their cameras, they agreed to give it a try. They removed the hot-mirror filter from my camera and had a piece of clear glass ground down to the exact dimensions to match. This modification cost $125 and was worth every penny. The results were truly amazing!

With the hot-mirror removed, the images with the number 87 opaque filter were almost too extreme for my taste. I started experimenting with other filters

Image by Tony Zimcosky.

to find a combination that better suited my needs. I used a number 25 red filter but still thought the infrared recording of the scene was too intense, so I ended up with an orange filter in front of the lens. You can decide what infrared "look" is best for your studio and then choose a filter accordingly.

With the orange filter in place, the digital infrared images look almost exactly like they were made on Kodak HIE infrared film—but with several distinct advantages. First, Kodak HIE infrared film is expensive ($12–$18 per roll). Second, with the LCD screen, you know instantly if you got the shot you wanted—there is no more need to bracket exposures. Third, with the camera modified, my shutter speeds are faster and I have less problems with subject movement during the exposure. Fourth, it is possible to modify almost any digital camera by having its hot-mirror filter replaced. You can choose to have a more expensive digital camera with a much larger file size modified for infrared imaging. Remember, however, that this modification will severely alter the images recorded in the color mode. Your color imaging will no longer record correctly. A modified camera effectively becomes useless except for infrared image recording.

Troubleshooting. The following are a few hints and tips that answer some of the most common questions photographers have when creating digital infrared images.

- The lower the existing light level, the longer the exposure, and the more likely you will be to have camera shake. When you compose your photographs, you must lock in the center on your subject or the image will focus beyond your subjects. Once you lock focus, you can then recompose your photo.

- When you view an image in the playback mode on the Nikon Coolpix 950, you can check to see what your actual exposure was by turning the finger wheel on the top right side of the camera. If your shutter speed was too long, you probably experienced camera shake.

- If you used a piece of red gel material for your filter, try also cutting a piece of orange material in a circle to use when you have less light. If that does not work, try yellow-orange. Your results will have somewhat less of the infrared effect, since you are blocking less of the visible spectrum of light with less red filters.

Image by Patrick Rice.

- When examining your images in Photoshop, it is normal to have to adjust the levels of the dynamic range of the image. This is because the center-weighted metering of the camera reads the white reflectance of the bride's gown and gives the image ½ to 1 stop less light than it may need. By moving the right delta on the levels scale to where the histogram begins to show information, you brighten up the image and make the whites cleaner. You will probably also have to move the left delta on the levels scale to bring up the black point so

Image by Patrick Rice.

The possibilities are endless and the results speak for themselves.

that the blacks in the image are richer looking. This quick levels adjustment is usually all that is needed to have dynamic digital infrared photographs.

- We have made digital infrared photographs from the Nikon Coolpix 950 camera up to 20x24 inches. However, because of the relatively small file size of the camera, we add noise in Photoshop as we make enlargements. For 8x10-inch images, we usually add 5 points of noise. For 11x14-inch images we may add 5 points twice. We find adding noise in smaller amounts two or three times looks better than adding a lot of noise all at once. Each image is different, so you need to look at the preview button in Photoshop to determine how much noise looks good to you.

Digital Infrared without a Digital Camera. If you are searching for the "look" of infrared, but do not want to create it with a digital camera as explained above, there is an alternative. A photographer named Fred Miranda offers an inexpensive downloadable infrared action for Photoshop that roughly simulates an infrared image. I purchased his action as a download directly from his web site (www.fredmiranda.com) for only $8.50. After loading the action into my Photoshop actions menu, I was able to quickly and easily convert any digital image into an infrared-like image.

There are, however, some subtle differences between using an infrared action and actually recording a scene in infrared with proper filtration. Most notably, the infrared action does not render clothing in the same way as Kodak infrared film or digital infrared capture. One of the qualities of true infrared that I have found very appealing is the differences in infrared reflectance of different materials. Black tuxedos with synthetic trim are very striking because the jackets and pants may record black, while the piping and trim are nearly white. Tuxedos that are made entirely of synthetic materials will record in gray or even white.

True infrared can even detect a person's real hair color. Sound strange? We photographed a bride with beautiful blonde hair only to have her hair record in infrared as dark gray. When I asked the bride about her natural hair color, she confirmed that she had her hair dyed blond. I have also seen infrared images where a subject has dyed their hair a dark color to try to hide gray hair. You can't hide from infrared. Infrared actions will never be able to magically "see" like true infrared can. Infrared capture from film or with a modified digital camera is still my personal choice.

The possibilities are endless and the results speak for themselves. The ability to still provide my clients with infrared images from their wedding day, a signature part of our film coverage of the event, makes the digital transition possible for my studio. I feel it is important for photographers to embrace the changes in technology and look for new and better ways to give their clients a unique product.

■ A PROFESSIONAL PERSPECTIVE
Digital Infrared Wedding Photography, by Tony Zimcosky

As a wedding photographer for over twenty years, I have observed that today's brides and grooms are much more demanding than they once were. At the studio that I work for, Rice Photography, we have been adding additional styles and techniques to the traditional wedding day coverage. About ten years ago, the studio began using black & white infrared film routinely on most weddings. The clients loved the photos, but it certainly added more work for the photographer. The client's expectations were very high, so we always bracketed each pose to ensure that it would turn out properly. This meant that I was juggling another camera and having to fire off three or four additional images of a pose that I also had to record with my medium format camera in color. This was while I was adjusting the camera settings for each image and watching the light each time. It was time-consuming and sometimes even nerve-racking.

When we began using digital cameras for the infrared wedding photography, my life got a lot easier. The cameras we use, modified Nikon Coolpix 950 and 990 models, couldn't be simpler. They are small and fit on a thin strap around my neck during the outdoor portion of the wedding day imaging.

What is great about these cameras is that the exposures are made automatically by the camera— all I have to do is turn them on and shoot! The exposures are always perfect and I get to see each image on the back of the camera's LCD screen. Digital infrared has uncomplicated my life as a wedding photographer. I would never want to go back to shooting infrared film on a wedding again.

Images by Tony Zimcosky.

DIGITAL WORKFLOW

Image by Scott Gloger.

Digital workflow for the photographer does not have to be as complicated and time-consuming as some photographers purport. Many digital photographers have established very simple workflow procedures that keep them from being bogged down by overwhelming and unnecessary image-handling methods.

▣ A SIMPLE DIGITAL WORKFLOW

Our studio employs very simple digital workflow procedures. Our images are written onto Compact-Flash cards by the camera at the time of image capture. If it is a wedding, the cards are held until they arrive back at the studio. We do not spend time downloading CompactFlash cards at the wedding or trying to write CDs when we should be creating images for the bride and groom.

Burning a CD. When we return to the studio, each CompactFlash card used on the wedding day is written to a CD as raw or uncorrected camera files. No manipulation, editing, etc., is performed. These files are exactly how the camera captured them. The CDs are labeled with the client name, wedding date, and the photographer's name. If there were two photographers on the wedding, each photographer's images would be on a separate CD. All digital infrared images are written to a separate CD, since they are captured on a separate Nikon Coolpix camera. We label each CD with a special marking pen designed for writing on CDs, so the ink won't bleed into the data and corrupt any of the files.

Some studios have chosen to write their images to DVD. The price of DVD writers for computers has dropped dramatically and the price of DVDs themselves has also become more reasonable. This can be especially useful for studios that shoot several hundred or even thousands of images at each wedding. DVDs can minimize the studio's disk storage because of their considerably larger storage capacity. Theses CDs or DVDs become the "negatives" for all of the images. The original CD is never altered and never leaves the studio.

Proofing. If we are making proofs for the client, we copy the images from the raw file CD, make any needed changes and corrections to them, and write these images to a new CD. The corrected copy is then sent to the color lab for the proofing. This is important because we no longer have to be concerned about something happening to our images. With film, the rolls could be lost or damaged in transit to the lab. Furthermore, once the film safely arrived at the lab, it could be lost or damaged there as well. We have all had experiences where a roll of film came up missing or an equipment problem damaged some of the film. When the proofs are returned from the lab, this proofing CD is retained in the client file, along with the raw CD as a backup.

Image by Penny Adams.

Orders. When orders are placed, another CD is written with the changes and corrections made to the images. This third CD is then sent to the lab for the necessary enlargements. Once returned, this CD is also placed in the client file. We now have a permanent history of each image presented to the client and what they looked like. This system is far superior to film, because with film the same negatives are used over and over throughout the process.

◼ A PROFESSIONAL PERSPECTIVE

Workflow in the Digital Environment, by Penny Adams

The workflow we use in our studio is primarily through computers. We have both Macintoshes and PCs. My preference is to use the Macintosh computers, as I feel that they are better suited to image control—but I'm also more comfortable with a Mac; I've been using one for almost twenty years.

Archiving Original Images. We capture the images on 256MB CompactFlash cards in the large JPEG resolution. I recognize that the JPEG (lossy) compression is not as ideal as shooting in the raw mode, but we feel that the quality is sufficient for our purpose. Once I get home from the event or session, the images are downloaded onto one of our Mac G3 computers. We then go through the images using the slide show option in JPEG View, a Macintosh-based graphics program, making a list of the "outs" and moving them to a separate folder (I don't throw away any images!). We then burn two copies of all the original images on CD. This may seem like overkill, but CDs can be damaged and they do degrade over time. After we verify that each CD can be read we put them into a special ring binder file of all our events. The digital images are then transferred to our PC, loaded into the ProShots software and sent to the lab via the Internet. ProShots is only available for PCs, which necessitates this transfer.

Since we still do some capture on film, the film is mailed to our lab for processing and ProShots scans. They make these scans available to us via the Internet, and I have them mail us a CD of the scans as well, which we file with the digital masters.

Web Album. The film-based scans are then merged with the digital scans and we create a "web album" for our clients. This isn't an album in the sense of a final, deliverable product for the couple. It is a compilation of all of the photographs of the day, grouped in a logical sequence. This becomes a series of pages on a web site that is hosted through Kodak's ProShots program and is linked to from a page on our web site. The "web album" allows our clients to share their images with their friends and family through the Internet.

The sales pitch from ProShots was that this would dramatically increase our sales. It hasn't—at least not in the way that was intended. We sell very few prints through the web, but we constantly have people saying that it is a wonderful way of getting to see the images. Typically, I hand out a card at weddings, saying that the images will be available two weeks from that day. There have been times when, due to some technical issues with either our Internet connection or at the hosting site, we have been late by a day. When this occurs (thankfully on a very

Images by Penny Adams.

infrequent basis), we will receive multiple calls asking where they are. The program is that popular! In fact, we've made sales simply because people have seen someone's wedding on the web and loved the concept.

Image Presentation and Album Design. We use Montage to plan the wedding albums and to present the images to portrait clients. They are currently shown on a 52-inch television that is connected to one of our computers. The resolution is quite poor when compared to monitor quality display, and we are in the process of upgrading to a digital projector which will provide a dramatic improvement. We preplan all our wedding albums before the client comes in, and then let them make any changes they want from there. While this does present more work on our part, it has also significantly increased our sales, since it makes the clients more aware of the design possibilities with the albums. Following up on the very first lessons we learned in Marketing 101, it's also very difficult for a bride to agree to take a picture out of her album once she sees it there!

Image Ordering. Once the clients have made their final choices, we input their order into ProShots and e-mail the order to our lab. Pro-Shots makes it as easy to place our digital orders as it does for our film orders. We do find that we are struggling

Image by Penny Adams.

with getting consistent color and quality results from our digital images. I feel this is because we are still working on the way we capture the images, and also because the labs are still working out their own workflow issues. The overall process is quite young, and labs and photographers are just beginning to learn how best to work with the many aspects of digital photography and printing. There are so many variables, certainly more than with film capture, that the learning process is more difficult, or at least different than what our traditional training has been. It takes time to work through these. While it seems like new issues crop up daily, the rewards of working in the digital medium greatly outweigh the problems.

◼ A PROFESSIONAL PERSPECTIVE

Digital Wedding Workflow, by Jeff and Kathleen Hawkins

Once you are offering a state-of-the-art digital experience to your clients, you need to begin implementing the digital process into your daily workflow. Beginning during the reception, here is the procedure we follow to deliver images to the client:

WEDDING DAY

1. Download images from camera to laptop and FireWire hard drive.
2. During dinner, get ready for the slide show.

Image by Jeff Hawkins.

3. Begin the continuous-play slide show on TV, laptop, or LCD projector during reception.
4. Print up and package gift items (frames, etc.) for presentation at the reception.

MONDAY

1. Prepare CDs immediately.
2. Download images to main computer from the FireWire hard drive and delete laptop folder.
3. Copy images into work folder. The original files are not touched until image ordering takes place.
4. Create a numbering system broken down into sections.
5. Personalize images with photo-manipulation software.
6. Create three duplicate digital proofing videos or DVDs.

TUESDAY THROUGH FRIDAY

1. Display a minimum of twenty images online.
2. Select and order stock photos for vendors.
3. Send the client an e-mail notifying them that their images are online and recommending that they schedule an album design session. Leave a telephone message as well.
4. Work on other Montage album orders.

◼ FUJI'S STUDIOMASTER PRO

StudioMaster PRO is an image presentation and ordering system that replaces crop cards and negatives with the convenience of using digital files. You can view, edit, create, present, and order images through one user-friendly system that enables you to gain control of your workflow while increasing your sales and customer satisfaction. You can create and view real album layouts on-screen, use it as a sales presentation tool, view and edit high-resolution images, and easily order images from your lab.

StudioMaster PRO: The Ultimate Pro–Lab Interface, by Michael Ayers

There have been many new ways to communicate digital orders to labs in the past few years, but none have the potential to be all things to all photographers like Fujifilm's StudioMaster PRO. My professional processor, H&H Color Lab (Raytown, MO), uses a host of digital printing equipment, including Fujifilm's Frontier printers, which are widely considered state-of-the-art in the industry. Utilizing the StudioMaster PRO software allows me the ability to virtually operate the lab and its printers from my studio's computer. I can control everything about my images including quantities, sizes, cropping, color balance, overlays, borders, black & white, retouching, and even "smart" album pages! StudioMaster PRO has a hundred little special features that allow me to be more efficient and save money. I can upload an order on a Monday morning and have the prints back as soon as Wednesday—without any rush charges! Many pro labs around the country are utilizing StudioMaster PRO, but it's advantageous to become a regular customer with just one good lab. During my lectures, I have

Image by Michael Ayers.

Image by Patrick Rice.

always stated that the first thing an aspiring pro should do is "get married" to a professional lab.

◼ KODAK PROSHOTS

Several years ago, when the Hicks Company first introduced the Pro-Shots software, we were one of the first studios to try it. Back then, we were a film-based studio and decided to use ProShots for the program's image-ordering feature. Allowing the clients to view and compare the images was a tremendous innovation in selling photographs. Furthermore, the lab maintained the negatives on a continuous roll at their facility so all we had to do was fax in the image number, size, and quantity desired. It really couldn't be easier. This completely alleviated the problem of negative storage for current customers and greatly expedited the ordering process by eliminating the time to mask negatives and then ship them to the lab.

The program further evolved into an even more powerful selling tool when the album-ordering feature was introduced. Now, the clients could view their prints in album mats just as they would appear in their finished wedding album. This boosted album orders by encouraging couples to choose more images to maintain the storytelling aspect of their wedding album.

Today, ProShots is owned by Kodak and has grown into an exceptional tool for any studio. Photographers can shoot with film or digital capture and can have all of their images posted online with a sales interface for orders over the web. The album feature not only helps your brides and grooms make the right selections for their book, it also can be used as a virtual album on the web for prospective clients to view your work. All in all, ProShots can save you time and help you make more money from every wedding.

DIGITAL OUTPUT

Digital output is probably the biggest area of concern for today's buyers of photography. As digital imaging evolved, two unique problems occurred with regard to digital output. First, many early digital cameras had too small a file size to make adequate quality enlargements. Both consumers and photographers were trying to enlarge digital images beyond the point of acceptability. This is somewhat similar to excessive film grain with 35mm enlargements—except that the pixelization from over-enlarging digital images is far less attractive. The second early problem with digital output was the quality of the printers that were available to both professionals and consumers. The inks on early inkjet printers were not very true to the color in the scene, and the papers that the prints were created on did not last. In other words, the images might fade or shift colors over time. Digital output turned many people off to digital imaging.

Today, this is all changed. First of all, it is not necessary for the professional photographer to print any of his digital images. Just about every professional color lab on the globe now accepts digital files and makes prints on Kodak or Fuji photographic paper. Moreover, these labs use the same machines in many cases to print either film files or digital files. This is a very important selling point when we discuss digital imaging with the clients. Some clients have the misunderstanding that their digital prints will not last. This is due in part to experiences with early inkjet prints and in part by misinformation from publications and photographers. Once our clients know that, whether their images are shot on film or digital, the same Fuji Frontier Printer will generate their proofs and enlargements and print them on the same Fuji Crystal Archive Paper, they are much more comfortable with the fact that we are a digital studio.

▢ PRINTING IT YOURSELF

Many studios, including ours, have found the need to own in-house printers for specific applications. When you calculate the cost of ink cartridges, paper, waste, and time, however, the prints that we make in-house cost *more* than sending the files to the lab for prints. In addition, professional color labs are more consistent in color and density than most photographers will be in-house. I have known several photographers who have attempted to print some of a bride and groom's 8x10-inch prints themselves on their inkjet printer, only to have the couple reject the images for lack of quality when compared to a lab print. As with any photo-

Digital output is probably the biggest area of concern for today's buyers of photography.

graphic print, the real test is when they are compared to another print from the same event that was printed on a different machine or paper.

New-generation inkjet printers are very good and are capable of making quality images. However, for consistency, the photographer must maintain proper calibration of their monitor and profiles of their printers. A profile is a description of the characteristics of a device that is used by other devices to manage or alter their own behavior. Profiles can be tagged or imbedded onto a data file so that as the data file is opened, devices compliant with that particular profile can read the imbedded information and utilize it to interpret the data.

Although I have met some photographers who print their own 4x5-inch or 4x6-inch proofs, this is not a cost-effective way to produce proofs. Many of the larger discount and department stores can produce proofs from a Fuji Frontier Printer on Fuji Crystal Archive paper at a cost of $.20–$.40 each with turnaround times from one hour to next day. Professional color labs have also become more competitively priced in the area of digital proofing. As a result, your color lab can produce your proofs for far less money than you can yourself.

Dye sublimation (dye-sub) printers produce very fine quality digital images that are superior to all but the best inkjet printers. We have used a small Canon CD 300 dye-sub printer for many years to produce quick digital prints at wedding receptions. We select one digital image from the wedding-day images and print three copies of it. This printer produces a very high quality 4x6-inch print, which we trim to 4x5 inches and place

Image by Mark Bohland.

inside a folder with our studio logo imprinted on it. We then present these portrait miniatures to the bride and groom and each set of parents during the dinner. The reaction is always one of amazement and appreciation. The images are passed around the room from guest to guest, which certainly helps us to secure more work in the future. The bride and groom also have an image from their special day to take with them on their honeymoon. Our cost is about $1 per print and $.50 per folder. It is certainly worth the modest investment for the positive public relations value!

▣ EPSON INKJET PRINTERS

In our studio, we have used the Epson line of printers for many years. The reproduction quality of their printers is very impressive, and the printers themselves just keep getting better. We used the Epson 2000P printer very successfully when we needed prints in a hurry. The only disadvantages of the 2000P were that it was somewhat slow to make a print and that we used up color ink cartridges very quickly. We got great images, but they were expensive. The inherent problem was that if a print had a large amount of a particular color in it, and you made several prints, the ink cartridge would be drained of that color, and the printer would indicate the need to change the color cartridge.

Epson solved this problem with the introduction of the Epson 2200 printer. The Epson 2200 uses separate color cartridges instead of just one color cartridge like the Epson 2000P. With seven different color cartridges, you simply replace the individual cartridge when it is empty—not the entire color cartridge.

In addition, black & white prints look much better on the Epson 2200 because of the specific black ink cartridges created to match the paper chosen. The Epson 2200 is also faster than the Epson 2000P printer, which is always a benefit for the photo studio in a hurry to deliver prints.

Our primary use for the Epson 2200 printer is to make prints quickly. Sometimes a client needs an image "right now," and this printer is perfect in that application. Also, if we miss an image from an order for the client from a portrait or wedding, we can print up the photograph ourselves instead of holding up the entire process by having to send the file back to the lab for an enlargement. Every studio should have one of these inexpensive printers to help them out in similar situations.

Images by Michael Ayers.

◻ A PROFESSIONAL PERSPECTIVE

Fuji Pictrography 4500: Better, Faster, Less Expensive, by Michael Ayers

About a dozen years ago, long before the advent of digital technologies for professional photographers, Fujifilm invented a system for making photographic-quality prints without inks—just distilled water. This invention is now in use in two studio-grade printers called the Pictrography 3500 and the Pictrography 4500. Both Fujifilm printers are fully self-contained, are Mac and PC compatible, and are priced to sell, starting at just a few thousand dollars.

The beauty of my 4500 printer is that it fills a gap between Eventpix.com and my local color lab. If I have a family in my studio for a portrait session, I can print them a quick contact sheet and take immediate orders (and get paid in full) on the spot. I also sometimes use the printer to make instant glossy black & white publicity portraits for media use. I can have a busy executive out the door in minutes with archival stable prints (without using a darkroom). What a power tool! Because I'm the only game in town with a

Pictrography 4500, I can also charge a nice price. Of course, when family members are scattered all over the country, it's still more profitable to use Eventpix.com, and all my final prints and enlargements are still made for my customers at my color lab.

From a marketing standpoint, my studio power tools not only allow me to generate and perform more business, they also allow me the chance to get my life back. With digital capture, too many of us live life behind a computer. Refining your workflow with these and other tools makes your studio more efficient and recession-proof, generates happier clients, and leaves your competition in the dust.

▣ A PROFESSIONAL PERSPECTIVE

The NetPrinter from Gretag: Your Own Digital Lab, by Jeff Smith

When I started in photography, I was like most young photographers. I used black & white film and then took over one of my mother's bathrooms to develop all the film I shot. My black & white dark-room/bathroom eventually turned into a color darkroom. At that point, I was sixteen, but I realized that for every hour I spent doing what I wanted to do (taking pictures), I spent three hours developing them.

Once I opened my studio, I found that poverty kept me in the darkroom, because I couldn't afford to send my black & whites to a lab. The happiest day of my life was when we finally had enough money to start sending *all* of our work to an outside lab. I washed the chemicals off my hands for the last time and never looked back.

The next fifteen years of my life without a darkroom was a pleasant time. Then, like many photographers, I made the decision to go digital. Unfortunately, the lab that had provided me with years of beautiful printing from negatives started giving me skin tones that did not exist in nature. Blue hair and purple skin wasn't the look that we were going for.

In addition to the problems of quality with the digital images we received from our lab, there was the cost of working on the digital files. With negatives, we cut the negatives, marked our order, and sent it off to the lab. The next time we saw the order it

Image by Jeff Smith.

was beautifully finished and ready to package. If it wasn't perfect, we simply marked it "remake" and sent it back. We were charged for each service, like negative retouching, mounting, and spraying, but with the volume of two studios, the prices were very competitive. With digital, that's all changed.

Image by Jeff Smith.

With digital we had to take over doing all the lab's work, with the exception of hitting the print button, and were were charged the same price for digital output as printing from negatives. This meant our lab bill was going to stay the same, but I would have to employ additional people to get all the files ready for the lab. As a businessperson, I didn't see the logic in handling my digital files that way.

I started having impure thoughts, thoughts about going back to something I never wanted to do again. While I was in no hurry to open up a lab, the cost of the time spent dealing with digital images made it a realistic option. I had to hire additional employees anyway, so why not use the profit that our lab made from our work to help pay for them? In theory, it sounded good, but it had been a long time since I worked in a darkroom, and I was in no hurry to have the smell and mess in my studio again.

After talking with photographers and equipment companies, I was convinced that I didn't need to have the mess and smell of a photographic processor. Everyone told me of the spectacular results that photographers were achieving with various types of printing devices. I also learned that photographers, as a group, are some cheap people—if there's a way to save a buck, even if quality suffers, they will give it a try!

After some research, I found that we had three options, and two weren't really options. Some photographers have been using ink-type printing devices. While the image quality looks impressive, the durability and feel of the product leave clients with a print that they could produce at home. We use ink printers for quick jobs that are for publication—prints that will not be handled frequently and only need to last for a short period of time. Call me old fashioned, but I don't feel comfortable delivering a senior photograph that will hang in my client's home for thirty years printed in this way.

The second option was one that we tried many years ago for printing our yearbooks. While dye-sub printers have improved (with lower output costs and faster printing times) they are still much more expensive than printing on photographic paper, and are still very slow for a high-volume business. Although the cost of the printers isn't as much as the photographic type printers, multiple machines would be needed to keep up with the workflow.

The third option seemed like the perfect solution: digital printers that actually printed on photographic paper using a CRT. I had seen the Fuji Frontier and some of the other printers in that same price range—really nice, but really expensive. I wanted to start a lab and actually pay for the equipment before it became obsolete.

We were at a trade show and I saw a digital printer/paper processor. I looked at it and watched a demonstration—and I got excited. The unit was a NetPrinter from Gretag. The NetPrinter, like other digital printers from other manufacturers, is a self-contained printer/processor that prints on almost any photographic paper. Our NetPrinter prints up to a 12x18-inch print at 500dpi. The average cost for an 8x10-inch image is $.35–$.45, and the NetPrinter can create about two hundred prints per hour. That's not bad, even with our volume. With this machine, I saw a way to pay for all those extra employees.

I wanted to start a lab and actually pay for the equipment before it became obsolete.

The first three months after installing the machine, I was having darkroom flashbacks, but without the smell. (You can purchase odorless chemistry now!) It wasn't nearly as easy as we expected it to be. Printing on the machine, which is loaded with ICC profiles for most popular digital papers, got us up and running quickly, but getting consistently acceptable results took some time. We purchased the EyeOne calibration software to calibrate each monitor and write specific ICC profiles for the machine. This got the monitors close to the final output on paper, but we had to learn to interpret the subtle differences between the colors and contrast of the monitor and how they reproduce on a specific paper. We also found that the machine produced much better results with certain types of papers than with others.

We are now going on a year with our lab. The staff is trained to interpret color, the customers are happy, and I have actually stopped taking orders home to work on at night. The additional costs, which would have been my lab's profit, have stayed in the studio to pay for our trained employees. For our studio, this was a necessary step to make digital as profitable as shooting with film.

When shooting digital, controlling costs becomes very important. While most photographers are excited about digital right now, I don't think that many are considering how much of their "free time" is being taken up preparing orders for a lab that is charging them the same amount as for film orders. Why would you raise your cost, reduce your profit, and work more hours to change from film to digital?

Image by Jeff Smith.

In my travels, I have heard photographers talk about the huge sales that digital has brought into their studios, paying for all the additional cost involved with

Cindy

Image by Jeff Smith.

shooting digital. When you look at the way in which they show their clients their images and the sales process they use with their clients, though, it is exactly the same as they did with film. They create proofs, present the proofs in a week, and hope for an order. I have to ask, if everything is the same, how are sales going to increase to cover the additional wages, equipment, constant upgrading of that equipment, and all the free time that you as the business owner must give up? I don't think the special-effects images are going to increase sales quite that much. As your costs go up (which any photographer who has done an analysis of film vs. digital will tell you), you have to look for ways to pay for those additional costs. I can say that the addition of our lab has made it possible to create higher profits from digital than were possible with film.

The NetPrinter takes care of a lot of our printing needs up to the standard size of 11x14 inches. Since we only work with seniors, that makes up about 95 percent of our printing needs. For larger prints, we still use an outside lab, but we send the order out with a sample 8x10-inch print for color matching.

As we prepared our lab, there were many services that required specific machinery. Most photographers never think about die cutting. The die cutter that "kiss cuts" wallets is a simple looking machine, but it costs over $4000. With film, we used to have the lab texture our proofs to make them more difficult for clients to scan and reproduce. This texture machine costs over $2000. I was quite surprised by the cost of many of these items. We sat down and figured out which we could live without to stay within budget. For those items we needed, we shopped on e-Bay, and purchased from used-equipment companies for bargains. The services and equipment we could live without, we put on a list to purchase someday, like after the NetPrinter is paid for.

I am often asked at what point an in-house lab is an option for a studio—or how high your studio's lab bill needs to be before you consider it. To that I say, "It depends on your lab!" When some photographers talk about how much they pay for their lab work, I am amazed. There is no golden number or ideal volume. I would consider an in-studio lab a viable option when one year's lab bill would equal the cost of putting in the lab. At this point, the lab will pay for itself before the equipment becomes obsolete. Some photographers might find

Image by Jeff Smith.

it feasible with a lower lab bill, and some might find it doesn't make sense even with a much higher bill—you have to do the math. As always, you should also talk to your accountant about major purchases and the tax advantages of leasing vs. purchasing before making any decisions.

Over the past thirty years, photographers have looked for ways to get the labs out of their studios, sending their work to an outside lab and focusing on what makes them the most money. Labs became better and better at providing services for competitive pricing, adding to this trend. With digital, this trend will be changing. More digital companies are entering into the market that serves the studio-owned lab, and more studios are finding it necessary to bring the lab back into their studios to make digital as profitable as film.

IMAGING SOFTWARE

While starting with a good original is as important for digital photography as it was for film, the original capture is more than ever just the starting point. With powerful software tools like Adobe Photoshop, images can be enhanced and perfected by the photographer in ways that were prohibitively time-consuming, expensive or just plain impossible with traditional materials and processes. The following sections are examples and step-by-step techniques for some of the most popular digital effects used in wedding and portrait photography. Use them as a starting point to designing images that match your creative vision.

▣ A PROFESSIONAL PERSPECTIVE
How I Create Digital Photo Art, by Robert Kunesh
I usually start with a photo that appeals to me in some way. The image itself talks to me somehow, and together the image and I begin doing something. Each image is different, and we always begin differently.

I usually begin by starting Photoshop and importing the image that grabs me at the moment. Then I begin playing with that image by using the tools that feel appropriate at the time. There isn't a formula to follow. I think the process of creating digital art starts when the photo I select sends ideas out to me and I, in turn, play with these ideas. This is one of the freedoms Photoshop allows you, since you can experiment freely without fear and just undo anything that doesn't seem to be working. You can try an effect, modify it, undo it, try something else, undo that, etc., until the image tells you to stop. Of course, it's really not the image that's telling you to stop but your emotion, your comprehension of the image, and your unconscious sense of reality.

Let me try to explain it by actually doing it. At this very moment, I have pulled out a box of images that I have stored behind me and have chosen an image of a bride that I photographed in my studio about five or six years ago. I have just scanned the image into Photoshop. Now, I'm just looking at it, hoping it might suggest something. I just noticed that it has a "no. 5" in the lower right corner, and it needs to be trimmed along the right side and bottom edge. I use the cropping tool to make this edit (Image 1).

I now apply the Crystallize filter (Image 2), and then (my "Ancient Chinese Secret") I go to Edit>Fade. At this point I have many different options. I pick the normal mode and pull the slider back to about 50 percent (Image 3). I actu-

Image 1 by Robert Kunesh.

Image 2 by Robert Kunesh.

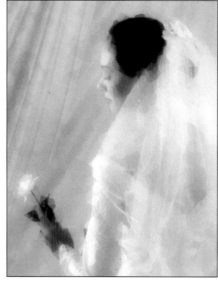

Image 3 by Robert Kunesh.

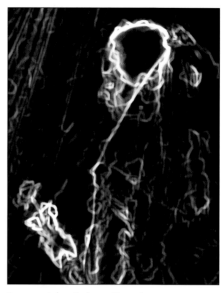

Image 4 by Robert Kunesh.

ally like the results and might just stop here—but, I don't. I decide to try another filter called Glowing Edges (Image 4). Interesting! But I go on to Edit>Fade and try one of the options. The result is Image 5. I actually go on to try another eight explorations with Image 6 being the last. I'll probably keep Image 3.

They say the average person comes up with two to three solutions to a problem, but the genius or the creative person comes up with at least ten. With Photoshop and a little imagination, you can probably come up with even more!

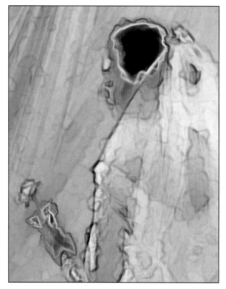

Image 5 by Robert Kunesh.

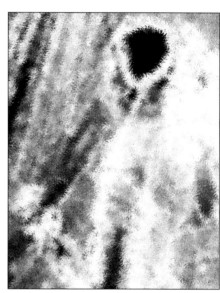

Image 6 by Robert Kunesh.

◼ PLUG-INS

In this ever-changing digital technology, one of the most exciting areas for photographers is the innovations in Photoshop plug-ins. Several different companies are making new and different software programs to make Photoshop an even more powerful tool. In our studio, we have absolutely fallen in love with the plug-in software by nik multimedia, Inc. The nik plug-ins are easy to use and can add many interesting effects to our digital image files.

We have probably examined and tested every method of black & white conversion of a color image and have found the nik filter equal to or superior to all of them. For a photographer that does not want to spend the time learning all of the different adjustments to make a quality black & white conversion, nik plug-ins are the answer. What we really like about this filter is that it allows us to make an adjustment to its default setting for total control over the manipulation process. In most cases, the software makes a perfect calculation of how much and to what extent everything should be adjusted.

Another filter by nik that we use quite often is the Monday Morning filter. This filter creates a soft and very moody rendition of any image. Again, we can make adjustments to fine-tune the image if necessary. The Pastel filter replicates the painterly pastel look in an image with amazing accuracy. The Sunshine filter can punch up a flat, low-contrast image. These are just a few of several filters that are included with each plug-in set. I am sure that each photographer will discover different ways to use these plug-ins to enhance their photography.

◻ A PROFESSIONAL PERSPECTIVE

Photoshop Actions, by Michael Bell

Actions are a powerful tool in Photoshop, allowing you to "script" a series of changes to an image and replay these changes on any image at the touch of a button. This works well for tasks where you need to do the same thing to many images. In the example that follows, you'll see how I create and use an action to make a basic image adjustment, convert my JPEG-format captures to TIF files, and save these files in a new folder. Why should you convert to the TIF format? Resaving images as JPEGs means that you will be losing additional data due to compression each time you save. Remember, JPEG is a "lossy" compression scheme, meaning that to save as a JPEG, the computer compares the data in the file and determines what data can be "thrown away" to reduce the file size. Then, the computer will "make up" the missing data when the file is opened. Doing so once, you lose data. Doing so again means you lose more of the data the computer has already determined to be good data, when it "throws away" more data to compress the file. Therefore, once I open a JPEG, I do not resave the file as a JPEG unless I really have to. I do, of course, retain the original JPEG files in a separate folder so that I can always come back to them if I should need the original file again.

This works well for tasks where you need to do the same thing to many images.

Before creating this action, I go to Window>File Browser and rotate my images as needed. To do this, select the thumbnail view for the desired image in the File Browser (if more than one needs to be rotated, just press the Shift key and click on as many files as you want). Then, hit "Control + [" to rotate the images to the left (counterclockwise) or "Control +]" to rotate the images to the right (clockwise). Photoshop only rotates the thumbnails until you open the files, then it opens and rotates the files. When you have completed this step, close the File Browser.

The next step is to record your action. Go to the actions palette and select New Action from the pull-down menu at the top right of the palette. Name the action as you like and hit the record button at the bottom of the palette (the round button). From this point on, any change you make will be recorded.

I prefer to record an action to do more than one thing. For example, I open one image, change the image size and resolution, and sometimes test the Auto Color or the Auto Levels (they don't always work, but in some cases they come close). Then I go to File>Save As and select the TIF file format, and save the image into a new folder, not back into the JPEG folder.

Having completed these steps, close the image and then press the square button at the bottom of the actions palette to stop recording.

To play the action, open another JPEG file, select the newly created action from the actions palette and hit play (the triangular button). Photoshop will rotate the file as you have selected in the File Browser, and the action will adjust the file, save it as a TIF, then close it.

Once the action is working, I go to File>Automate>Batch. With the following settings in place, this will cause Photoshop to open each of the images and apply the newly created action. At the top of the dialog box, I select my new action. Then I go to Source Folder, click on Choose, and point the way to the folder containing the JPEGs. For the Destination Folder, I click on Choose and point the way to the new folder where I want to store the resulting TIF files. For file naming, select Document Name + Extension. Make sure Stop for Errors is selected. That's it—just click OK.

This will cause Photoshop to open each of the images and apply the newly created action.

You can now go out for a Coke. If the JPEG folder has fifty images, Photoshop will run all of them and then stop. There is nothing to limit you as to how many files you can open, unless you run out of RAM. Photoshop should still try to open the files, even in this event, but it will be slow.

To make Photoshop run better, go to Edit>Preferences>Memory & Image Cache and set the Cache Levels to 4, unclick Use Cache for Histograms (this means that Photoshop will create histograms only when it needs them, not every time you open a file and use RAM). I set the percentage of RAM for Photoshop at 85 percent. If you do a lot of multitasking (with many programs open at once), then 85 percent is good; if you only run Photoshop and nothing else at the same time, you can set this up to 95 percent and speed up Photoshop. You also should be logged on to Windows XP or Windows 2000 Professional as a Power User, not as the Administrator. When you are logged on as the Administrator, Windows loads a lot of behind-the-scenes programs the administrator usually needs, but those programs hog RAM and slow down both Windows and Photoshop.

▣ A PROFESSIONAL PERSPECTIVE

Traditional Photographic Effects
with Adobe Photoshop, by Michelle Perkins

When many people think of digital image manipulation, they envision wild-looking composites and highly stylized photographs. While these effects are a lot of fun to play with, Photoshop is also an ideal tool for creating more traditional images. Instead of spending hours in the darkroom laboriously dodging and burning, you can now use the superior control offered by digital dodging and burning—and since every operation can be reversed, you'll never make an error that means starting over. With digital handcoloring, you can try color after color, in every intensity you can imagine, and will never need to start over with a new print. The steps below take you through three traditional techniques and show you how to create them in Photoshop. Keep in mind that you can adjust the settings and adapt the techniques to suit the image you are working on and achieve the effect you want.

Vignetting. Vignetting is a darkening (or, in some cases, a lightening) around the edges of an image. Sometimes this can occur accidentally (often from using a filter or lens attachment that is too small for the lens), but it is also done intentionally. The basic techniques for high key (light) and low key (dark) vignetting are detailed below.

Low Key Vignetting. Low key vignetting is probably the most common type. This technique is normally applied to images where the overall subject matter is normal to dark. It involves darkening the corners and sides of the image, making the central portion of the frame the lightest in the photo (and therefore the part the viewer's eye will be drawn to). The process is easy:

Image 1. (Original image by Jeff Smith).

Image 2.

1. Begin with a color or black & white image in the RGB or grayscale mode (Image 1). (*Note:* If you choose to work in the grayscale mode, you will only be able to create a grayscale vignette—this may be exactly what you want, but if not, convert your image to the RGB mode. You can convert it back later.)

2. The next step is more subjective and will vary from photo to photo. Using any of the selection tools (marquee, magic wand, lasso), select the area that will not be vignetted (i.e., the area that you want to remain untouched in the final image). Normally, this will be the subject of the photograph and some of the area around it. Your selection could be a square, circle, oval, rhomboid, a heart—anything you like (Image 2).

3. With your selection activated, invert the selection (Select>Inverse). This command will select everything that wasn't in your original selection. This is the area where the vignette will be created. If you've created any kind of complicated selection, or are just paranoid, you may want to save the selection so there's no danger of losing it accidentally. To do this, go to Select>Save Selection, and name your selection in the dialogue box. If you do accidentally deactivate your selection, you can then reload it by going to Select>Load Selection and choosing the appropriate name from the pull-down menu. Be sure to delete this selection (it will appear in the channels palette and can be dragged into the trash) when you are done. Otherwise, you will be prohibited from using the full range of file formats when you save your image.

4. With your selection still activated (but now inverted), feather the selection using the Select>Feather command (Image 3). Feathering blurs the edges of the selection so that the transition will be gradual between the vignetted and unvignetted areas of the image. You can decide how

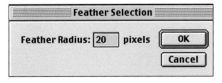

Image 3.

Image 4.

Image 5.

Image 6.

much feathering is needed for the effect you want. A few examples are shown above (Images 4–6). The only difference between these images is in the amount of feathering.

After it was feathered, the selected area was filled using the Edit>Fill command and selecting black with the blending set to 50 percent opacity. Keep in mind that feathering is resolution dependent. This means that that higher the resolution of your image, the more you'll need to feather the selection edge to create a soft appearance.

5. From this point you have a lot of options. A few variations are described below.

A. With the selection still activated, create a new layer (Layer> New>Layer). Use the Edit>Fill command to fill the selected area with the color of your choice. Reduce the layer opacity (Layer>Layer Style>Blending Options) to allow some of the underlying image to show through.

B. With the selection still activated, copy (Edit>Copy) and paste (Edit>Paste) the contents of the selected area of the image into a new layer. Using any of the tools under Image>Adjustments (curves, levels, variations, brightness/contrast, etc.), you can reduce, darken, or alter the color of the selected area. You can then set the opacity of this layer as you like (Layer>Layer Style>Blending Options).

C. With the selection activated, create an adjustment layer (Layer>New Adjustment Layer) of whatever type you like (curves, layers, etc.). Darken or otherwise adjust the vignetted area with this layer, then set the opacity of the layer as you like (Layer>Layer Style>Blending Options).

D. With the selection still activated, copy (Edit>Copy) and paste (Edit>Paste) the contents of the selected area of the image into a new layer. Experiment with the layer modes (Layer>Layer Style>Blending Options) to create whatever effect you like. Image 7 shows the use of the multiply mode at 100 percent layer opacity—a very natural effect.

Image 7.

E. With the selection still activated, use the burn tool to darken the vignetted areas as you like. Try different settings to burn primarily the highlights, shadows or midtones, and to alter the exposure. With the burn tool selected, the various options are all listed in the options menu at the top of the screen.

6. When you've created an effect you like, flatten the image (Layer>Flatten Image) and save it (save the unflattened version, too, if you think you might ever want to change it).

Image 8. (Original image by Jeff Smith.)

Image 9.

High Key Vignetting. High key vignetting is normally applied to images where the subject of the photo is the darkest thing in the frame (e.g., a polar bear eating a marshmallow on a snowbank). Even with images like these, dark vignetting may sometimes be more effective—use your judgment. High key vignetting involves lightening the corners and sides of the image, making the central portion of the frame the only dark area in the photo (and therefore the part the viewer's eye will be drawn to). The process is just as easy as creating low key vignetting:

1. Begin with a color or black & white image in either the RGB or grayscale mode (Image 8).

2. The next step is more subjective and will vary from photo to photo. Using any of the selection tools (marquee, magic wand, lasso), select the area that will not be vignetted (i.e., the area that you want to leave untouched in the final image). The selection can be any shape you like.

3. With your selection activated, invert the selection (Select>Inverse). This will select everything that wasn't in your original selection (the area where the vignette will be created).

4. With your selection still activated (but now inverted), feather the selection using the Select>Feather command. Feathering blurs the edges of the selection so that the transition will be gradual between the vignetted and unvignetted areas of the image. You can decide for yourself how much feathering you'll need to create the effect you want.

5. There are somewhat fewer options with lightening, presuming you are starting with an image that is already very light in the area to be vignetted. If, for some reason, you are applying a light vignette to a medium to low key image, refer to options B, C, and D on page 68, but use the same tools to lighten (rather than darken) the selected area. For those starting with a light image, two variations are described below.

A. With the selection still activated, create a new layer (Layer>New>Layer). Use the Edit>Fill command to fill the selected area with white (or perhaps another very light color). You may also wish to reduce the layer opacity (Layer>Layer Style>Blending Options) very slightly to allow some of the underlying image to show through (Image 9).

B. With the selection still activated, use the dodge tool to lighten the vignetted areas as you like. Try different settings to dodge primarily the highlights, shadows, or midtones, and to alter the exposure. With the dodge tool selected, these settings are all listed in the options menu that is located at the top of the screen.

Soft Focus. Soft focus is typically used in portraits (most often portraits of women) to create a softer, more flattering effect. This can help to hide the little flaws that most people don't want to see. Soft focus should not make the image seem blurry or out of focus; the image should be acceptably sharp, but with a softening of hard lines. Soft focus is normally achieved using either a special soft focus lens or soft focus filters attached to a regular lens. With Photoshop, you can achieve much more precise control and apply the soft focus look as selectively as you like.

Technique 1. The first technique allows you to "paint" softness onto an image exactly where you want it. This is a good technique for portraits where you want to soften only select areas (a few wrinkles, for example) but don't want a "soft focus" look on the entire image.

1. Begin with an image in the RGB or grayscale mode (Image 1).
2. Apply a Gaussian blur to the entire image (Filter>Blur>Gaussian Blur). Ten pixels is a good starting point (Image 2). If this gives you a look you are happy with, you can stop right here (Image 3). Most often (especially with portraits, where sharpness is especially desirable in the eyes), you will want to apply the effect more selectively. If so, proceed to the next step.
3. In the history palette, click on the box to activate the history brush icon next to the Gaussian blur state (Image 4). Then click on the "open" state in the history

Image 1. (Original image by Rick Ferro.)

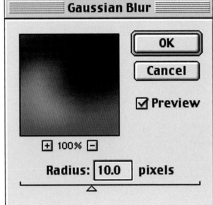

Image 2.

Image 3.

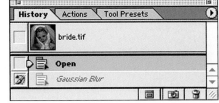

Image 4.

Image 5.

Image 6.

palette. The blur will disappear, but the Gaussian blur state will remain visible in the history palette.

4. Select the history brush and set it to the lighten mode in the history brush options menu. This will allow the brush only to blur dark into light, for a more subtle effect. Set the opacity of the history brush to 50 percent to start.

5. Select a soft brush. Next, simply "paint" on the soft focus effect wherever you want it. Image 5 shows an unsoftened area of this portrait. Image 6 shows that same area with softness painted on from the Gaussian blur history state.

Technique 1. If you want an equal degree of softness across the entire image, try the following method. This effect is also quite useful in cases where you want to apply equal softness to all but a very small part of the image. In that case, follow steps 1–5, then select the eraser tool and set its opacity to about 50 percent. Then, simply "erase" the areas in the duplicate layer where less softness is desired.

Image 7.

1. Begin with an image in the RGB or grayscale mode.
2. Duplicate the background image (Layer>Duplicate Layer). Click on the new layer in the layers palette to activate it.
3. Apply a Gaussian blur to the new layer.
4. In the layers palette, set the layer mode of the duplicate layer to lighten (image 7).
5. Since this effect is on a separate layer, you can adjust the layer opacity to reduce the softness as needed.

Clear Center Soft Focus. Clear center soft focus filters are also popular. These provide softening at the edges of the image, but not in the center. To achieve the effect digitally, turn to page 67 and follow steps 1–4 for vignetting. With your selection active, copy the selected area and paste it into a new layer. Next, apply a Gaussian blur to the new layer and set the new layer's mode to lighten. You can also adjust the layer opacity as you like.

Diffuse Glow. Although the result looks a little less like traditional soft focus, the Diffuse Glow filter is designed to create the look of a diffused image. To apply the filter, simply open an image in the RGB mode and go to Filter> Distort>Diffuse Glow. Adjust the sliders for Graininess, Glow Amount, and Clear Amount until you are satisfied, then hit OK (image 8).

Image 8.

Handcoloring. Handcoloring black & white photos (or color ones for that matter) is usually accomplished with a variety of artistic media—pastels, watercolors, oil paints, pencils, etc. However, if you've ever actually colored an image by hand, you know how much time it takes—and also how easily small mistakes can have you desperately trying to remove problematic colors with various solvents and bleaches. With Photoshop, the process is remarkably easy—and if you goof or change your mind you can just hit Edit>Undo (or use the history palette to backtrack if you didn't notice the problem right away). For those of you who never got the hang of coloring, you can create selections or masks to help you stay inside the lines. You can also try out lots of different looks and experiment freely with colors before deciding what works best.

Color Layers Method. Like most tasks, handcoloring in Photoshop can be accomplished in several ways: the use of layers in the color mode, the use of the the hue/saturation command, or by using the eraser tool on desaturated layers. We'll begin working simply with color layers, since this is the most intuitive method.

Image 1. (Original image by Rick Ferro.) Image 2.

1. Begin with an image in the RGB color mode (Image>Mode> RGB) (Image 1). The image must be in a color mode or you will not be able to add color to it. If you want to add hand-colored effects to the color image, proceed to step 2. For the more traditional look of hand-coloring on black & white, go to Image>Adjustments>Desaturate to create a black & white image in the RGB color mode (Image 2).

2. Create a new layer (Layer>New>Layer) and set it to the color mode (Image 3).

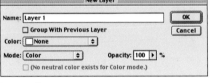

Image 3.

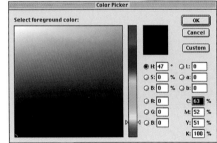

Image 4.

3. Double click on the foreground color swatch to activate the color picker (Image 4). Select the color you want and hit OK to select it as the new foreground color. This is the color your painting tools will apply. You may switch it as often as you like.

4. With your color selected, return to the new layer you created in your image. Click on this layer in the layers palette to activate it, and make sure that it is set to the color mode.

5. Select the brush tool and whatever size/hardness brush you like, and begin painting. Because you have set the layer mode to color, the color you apply with the brush will allow the detail of the underlying photo to show through.

6. If you're a little sloppy (as in Image 5), use the eraser tool (set to 100 percent in the options menu) to remove the color from anywhere you

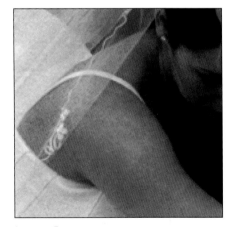

Image 5.

Image 6.

didn't mean to put it. Using the magnifying glass to zoom in tight on these areas will help you work as precisely as possible.

7. If you want to add more than one color, you may wish to use more than one layer, all set to the color mode.

8. When you've completed your handcoloring, the image may be either completely or partially colored. With everything done, you can flatten the image and save it as you like (Image 6).

Desaturating with Layers. Here's a quick way to add a handcolored look in seconds—or, with a little refinement, to avoid having to select colors to hand-color with. This technique works only if you are starting with a color image.

1. Begin with a color image in the RGB or CMYK mode.
2. Duplicate the background layer by dragging it onto the duplication icon at the bottom of the layers palette.
3. Desaturate the background copy (Image>Adjustments>Desaturate). The image will turn black & white—but by reducing the opacity of the desaturated layer you can allow the colors from the underlying photo to show through as much or as little as you like (Images 7–9).

Image 7 (40% layer opacity).

Image 8 (60% layer opacity).

Image 9 (80% layer opacity).

4. To create the look of a black & white handcolored image, set the opacity of the desaturated layer to 100 percent and use the eraser tool to reveal the underlying photo. Adjust the opacity of the eraser to allow as much color to show through as you like (Images 10–12).

Image 10 (20% eraser opacity).

Image 11 (40% eraser opacity).

Image 12 (60% eraser opacity).

5. If you make a mistake and erase an area you meant to leave black & white, you can use the history brush to paint the black & white back on from the desaturated history state.

6. For a very soft, desaturated look, set the opacity of the desaturated layer to about 90 percent (just enough to let colors show through faintly) and use the eraser tool (set to about 50 percent) to erase areas where you want an accent of stronger color to appear.

■ A PROFESSIONAL PERSPECTIVE

Photoshop Collages, by Rick Ferro and Deborah Lynn Ferro

Collages can be used for marketing purposes and for client images and album pages. For the photographer who competes at the local, state or national level, collages created in Photoshop for competition are becoming more and more the standard. Whether a single image with a mat and stroke is created or combined images are used, the possibilities are limitless.

In the example shown here, three images were combined. One was digitally handcolored and used as the background, while the others were converted to black & white and added to the collage. You can follow the steps below to create a similar collage using your own images.

Step A

1. To create the background image, begin by sizing the background image. It should be at the same size as your desired final print.

2. Make a copy of the background layer by dragging it onto the new layer icon at the bottom of the layers palette.

3. Desaturate the image by going to Image>Adjustments>Desaturate.

4. By adjusting the setting at the top of the layers palette, reduce the opacity of your saturation to bring back a little bit of the color. The result is softer than the original color image.

5. To add color to create a handcolored effect, select the brush tool and set it to the color mode (in the options bar). Set the opacity to 25 percent and set the foreground color as you like (click on the freground color to bring up the color picker, select a color from the Swatches palette, or adjust the sliders in the color palette). Then, color the petals of the bouquet.

Step B

1. Open the additional images to add to the background.

2. Crop the images to the desired size to fit on the background, keeping the resolution the same as the background.

3. Covert the images to black & white by going to Image> Adjustments>Desaturate.

4. If needed, use the levels or curves tool to increase the contrast in each image.

5. Flatten each image (Layer>Flatten Image).

6. Next, create a line (called a stroke) around each image. To do this,

Images by Deborah Ferro.

select the entire image by going to Select>All (or Ctrl+A for PC, Cmd+A for Mac). Then go to Edit>Stroke. The larger the number on the width setting, the wider the line around the photo will be. The stroke color will be set automatically to your foreground color. If you want to change it, click on the color swatch for the color. This will bring up the color picker. Since the selection line to which the stroke will be applied runs around the very outside edge of the photo, select Inside for the location of the stroke, so you will be able to see its full width.

7. Choose the move tool and drag each image into the background image file. You should now have three layers—one for the background, one for the bride, and one for the groom.

Step C

1. Position the images as you like.
2. Flatten the collage.
3. Sharpen the entire collage with the unsharp mask filter.
4. Save the finished image as a TIF file.

Collage by Deborah Ferro.

PRESENTING DIGITAL IMAGES TO YOUR CLIENTS

◻ TRADITIONAL PAPER PROOFS

With the advent of digital capture, the photographer now has several choices in the area of digital proofing. Of course, the studio can still have their color lab make 4x5-inch or 4x6-inch traditional paper proofs. This is what our studio still does for all of our wedding photography. The reason we have maintained traditional paper proofs is very simple; it has allowed a very smooth transition for our customers from film capture to digital capture. Many wedding clients are uneasy with the notion of not receiving actual photographs to view and select from their wedding day. By continuing to provide paper proofs, we can assure the clients that digital photography is just a means of image capture and does not impact what they receive from the studio. This puts their minds at ease and has made them more accepting of the technology.

Image by Barbara Rice.

Image by Barbara Rice.

For the studio, traditional paper proofs are a very inexpensive option. With discount and department stores making 4x6-inch proofs for just a few cents each, it is easy to build the small cost into the package. We find that including the proofs in our packages provides us with a distinct competitive advantage over studios that do not. Wedding photography is unique in that the clients always want to retain every image from the day. Unlike portraiture where the goal is to create one or two great images, wedding-day photography is a story that is only complete in its entirety.

DIGITAL CONTACT SHEETS

Many studios have chosen to create digital contact sheets containing multiple images on a single sheet of paper. These contact sheets provide a means for the client to view a rendering of the images for selection purposes. While most studios make their contact sheets on photo-quality paper, I have seen some studios just use regular copier paper. We create contact sheets for our portrait clients when it is not a viable option to have them select their images in our studio on our monitor. Many studios place an overlay of their studio name or logo on the images so that the client does not simply cut up the contact sheet and use the prints as finished images. Many album companies now offer three-ring binders to accommodate these digital contact sheets. These provide a professional appearance for the studio, especially if they are using the contact sheets for a wedding.

ONLINE PROOFING

Online proofing is yet another option for today's photographers. We offer online proofing of weddings and other special events in addition to paper proofing. Eventpix.com is our choice for online proofing because they charge an up-front fee of only $40 for large events and $10 for small events (under forty images). They host the images for a period of sixty days, and we have the option of extending that for a nominal fee.

Unlike other online hosting companies, Eventpix.com does not take a percentage of each sale. All orders are forwarded directly to our studio and all credit card information is secure. They even calculate shipping and sales tax. It simply couldn't be easier for the photographer.

We also chose to use this service because it allowed us to determine who makes our prints. Some twenty-five plus color labs are now directly involved with Eventpix.com, and more labs are scheduled to join. Many other online posting companies handle the entire transaction and make the prints. We were concerned about using one of these because it would limit our control over the consistency in color balance and image quality. We want all of our images to be printed from the same source.

▣ A PROFESSIONAL PERSPECTIVE

Eventpix.com: The Future of Ordering Photographs, by Michael Ayers
Welcome to the new millennium! As 21st-century image-makers, we will now be able to market ourselves as cyberspace ready, so start putting your images online and taking orders by e-mail today. A few years ago, in a desperate search to find the best online photographic ordering web site, I came across Eventpix.com—this is a company that is different from the rest in several ways. Eventpix.com asks for just a minimal up-front fee per upload; there is a massive limit of 1,000 images per event; the orders come securely and directly back to me with no sur-

Start putting your images online and taking orders by e-mail today.

Image by Michael Ayers.

charges; and the site is fast and easy for anyone to use on any computer. The best part is that I am now getting orders from clients all over the continent—many of whom would have never seen the photographs otherwise. During my busy wedding season, every time I go online I make more money without having to set up appointments or make phone calls. This powerful tool is summed up like this: upload, set prices, check e-mail, accept payment, and process orders. Easy!

◻ A PROFESSIONAL PERSPECTIVE
Online Proofing, by Jeff and Kathleen Hawkins

It's a good idea to offer a program to your customers charging them for placing their proofs online. Create a specific price for placing engagement proofs online and an additional price for wedding images.

We suggest that the number of the images, the selection of the prints, and duration of online visibility be selected at the discretion of the photographer. This way, you can select what is displayed, how long it will be displayed and how much it costs. For more information on online ordering, go to www.morephotos.com. The cost for this type of service is minimal and the response can be incredible.

Today, many couples can distribute an e-mail to all of the guests who shared their special day with instructions on how to view their images. If the old method of proofing is the only option, it is very unlikely they will ship proof books to every guest who attended their special day! As a result,

Image by Jeff Hawkins.

you will miss out on sales that going digital could have generated.

As a review, in order to market with digital finesse, you must begin by introducing your market to the digital age. As you develop this introduction process, you will also cultivate a style of digital selling. This will help you prepare your clients for the wedding-day benefit of digital, and adapt new your selling techniques to the advantages of the digital technology.

■ VIDEO PROOFING

Still other photography studios offer video proofing for their clients. This type of proofing has been popular for many years since many video cameras can cre-

ate a positive image from film nega-
tives. It was very easy for studios to create a video proof book for the clients by simply processing the film and using a Photovix or similar view-ing device. Creating video, CD, or DVD movies of a client's images can save the studio the expense of proof-ing and guard against illegal copying of the images. There are many soft-ware programs available for CD albums. We have used FlipAlbum because of its simplicity for both the photographer and the client.

■ A PROFESSIONAL PERSPECTIVE
Post-Session Proofing,
by Jeff Smith

When I first opened my studio, we showed family portraits on Trans-Vues, which were 35mm slides for-matted to fit the composition of the film you used. When we shot with Hasselblad, they came in a square, and when we switched to 645 they were rectangular. We had a long, nar-row living room setting and over the sofa we hung a 40x60-inch frame with a piece of white foamcore inside.

Image by Jeff Smith.

I'd show each pose in this 40x60-inch size. Since the projector had a zoom lens, we could project the images in three sizes. The idea was that the client got used to seeing the portrait in the 40x60-inch size and anything smaller just seemed "small." Additional sales were made because the slides didn't leave the stu-dio. The first time a client saw the portraits they'd become excited—and that excitement resulted in larger sales. This simple sales technique helped sell larg-er wall portraits and raised our profits from each session. Without this type of selling, I never would have made it through those first few lean years when I opened my studio.

Ever since I entered into professional photography, I've heard photogra-phers talking about the huge sales that were possible when all of the preview-ing was done in the studio. Instant previewing is one of the only reasons why many mall photographers/corporate studios are able to sell photos. People look at their photographs for the first time and place their orders. We have an emotional product and that product sells best when a client is still emotional about it.

Let's be honest—it's photographers, not clients, who have kept paper proofs around for so long. I think the reason is that the method is non-confrontational. When you (or a studio staff member) show the images after a session, there's some risk involved, a risk of rejection. The client could look at those portraits and say they're the ugliest images they've ever seen. He or she could say they could have done a better job with their own digital camera at home. The feelings photographers experience after hearing comments like this make them fearful of selling, and that's why so many still use paper proofs.

How many times have photographers looked at a session, realized they did less than their best job shooting it and, rather than confronting the client about reshooting, just taken the proofs, sealed the envelope, and handed them to the client? They only hope that the client will wait until they get home to open them so they don't have to deal with any problems in person. I know other photographers who mail proofs directly to their clients' homes.

Image by Jeff Smith.

Talk about shooting yourself in the foot—they have no chance to sell anything! They're relying on the quality of their images and a client who, like all of us, loves to put things off. They have to take time to read and understand a confusing price list, then they have to make time to come into your studio to place an order. Some clients will order, but many clients will simply put it off and forget. Photographers who live in fear of dealing with a dissatisfied client lose sales. Overcoming that fear is the greatest achievement—it's one of the best steps a photographer can take.

The popularity of another client favorite, digital proofs on CD, also stems from photographers who hate selling. When photographers send these photo CDs home with clients, their fear of confrontation shows— and overwhelms their good business sense. In our studio, we don't make paper proofs, and we don't offer our clients photo CDs, either. If I'm going to go through all the extra work and absorb the added costs that are involved with digital, I'm going to be well paid for it. If I don't increase my profit, I'll lose money by shooting a session with digital as opposed to film.

Working with digital gives us the perfect opportunity to have the client make a purchase right after the session. If a client asks for proofs, you can explain that when everyone used negative film a photograph had to be made for a client to see the image. With digital, you can see the image immediately, so a paper proof is unnecessary. A great follow-up to that statement is, "This is why we can have so many images to choose from in a digital session. This would be impossible with film because of the cost."

Have the client make a purchase right after the session.

Image by Jeff Smith.

MARKETING TECHNIQUES FOR DIGITAL IMAGES

Like all businesses, marketing is one of the keys to success for the photographic studio. Marketing digital imaging presents both challenges and opportunities to today's digital studio. The first thing that digital photographers must realize is that they are still in the minority. Many of the die-hard film studios are actually propagating negative marketing toward digital studios. These studios are actively bad-mouthing digital imaging through half-truths and misinformation. Digital photographers need to be aware of this and take proactive steps to not lose market share to traditional film-based studios.

■ ADVERTISING VS. MARKETING

Many photographers confuse advertising with marketing. The purpose of advertising is to let consumers know that you have a product or service available. Advertising is meant to get the phone to ring and produce more business. The purpose of marketing is to show the consumer that the product or service you offer is superior to that of your competition. Marketing is much more targeted and requires the studio to understand both their own products and services as well as those of their competition. We follow what our competitors do very closely so that we do not lose our competitive advantage in our area.

Image by Ken Holida.

■ A SUPERIOR PRODUCT

For our studio, we made up several samples of larger images that were all from digital capture. We display these images along with a couple of older film-capture images so that the clients can compare them to each other and see that they are not sacrificing any quality when their portrait is captured digitally.

We did the same thing in our wedding consultation room. Besides wall images, we mixed digitally captured 8x10-inch and 5x7-inch images into our sample albums. When we first converted to a strictly digital studio, I would challenge clients to identify which images were film capture and which were digital. They could not identify a difference. I even did this with some of my more skeptical colleagues. Even other professional photographers could not pick out the digital prints! This has proved to be very effective in disproving some of the misinformation from my competition.

In addition, we point out the advantages of digital photography over film. We do this both verbally when talking to the customer in person or on the phone, as well as with supplemental paperwork that is given to our potential clients. Especially with our wedding clients, we explain the tremendous value of digital photographers being able to see and review every image they record. This gives our clients peace of mind because they know their images will all turn out and turn out well. With film cameras, the photographer never knows exactly what they are recording until they get their proofs back. They never truly know if the camera was working properly or if their exposures were correct. Once the proofs come back from the lab, it's too late. This has always been a major concern with wedding clients and digital imaging eliminates that concern.

We also talk to our clients about how dramatically digital has improved over the last few years. File sizes are significantly larger, storage capacity has increased, and the cameras themselves perform better than models that are even a year old. We

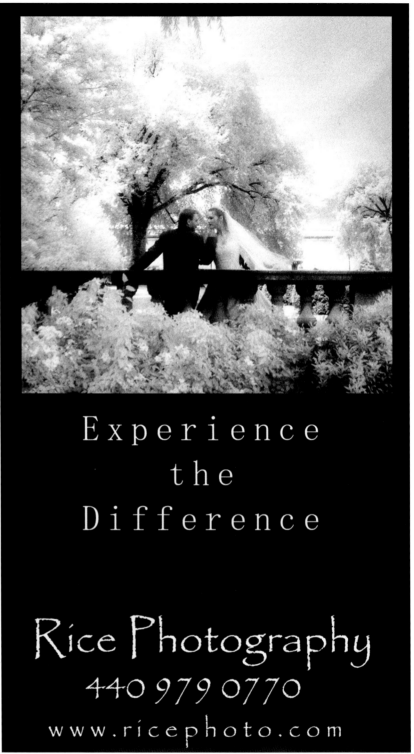

Promotional piece, Rice Photography.

also point out to our clients that the original image CD from their wedding or portrait session never leaves the studio. We make a copy of this original CD to send to the lab for proofing or enlargements, so they never need to worry that either the shipping service or the lab could damage or lose the film and everything will be gone forever. If the CD that we send out is lost or damaged, we just make another copy and send it off again. It is surprising how few clients think about this possibility and how relieved they then are when they know that we have eliminated it from consideration.

We further point out to clients that just because we are using digital capture does not mean that we make all of our own prints. We explain that the Fuji Frontier Printer can accept either negatives or CDs and uses the same lenses and paper for both. This is important because some film studios misinform clients by stating that digital prints will fade in a very short amount of time.

Finally, we point out that digital photographers tend to take more images during a photo session because of their ability to edit prior to the printing of any image. This provides the client with more and better choices from their session or wedding.

☐ THE IMPORTANCE OF YOUR WEB PRESENCE

For photographers today, the importance of a web presence cannot be overstated. The 21st-century bride is very Internet savvy, and the web has replaced the phone book as her directory of service providers. If you are not capable of making a dynamic web site for your studio, hire an individual or company who can. You only get one chance to make a first impression, and to many consumers, your web site is just that. Make the most of this impression!

Showcase Your Best Images. Your web site only needs a selection of your best work to really have a lasting impact on buyers of photographic services. In fact, I have seen great web sites for rather mediocre photography studios. These studios knew the importance of making a great first impression and showcased the best images they had.

Ease of Use. Your web site should load quickly and be easy to navigate. Too many photography web sites include extremely large files that take considerable time to load. Many potential clients will log off before they even get into your site if they are forced to wait too long. One of the advantages of the Internet is its speed. When people have to wait for long downloads, they get impatient and leave.

Images from the Rice Photography web site.

Images from the
Rice Photography web site.

Be careful not to get too fancy—especially on your opening page. Ease of navigation is an important consideration when designing a web site. Your buttons, boxes, or headings should be easy to understand and work with. Remember, the consumer wants information about your studio and what services you can provide. Give that to them in a fast and efficient manner, and your web site will increase your business.

Photographic Association Sites. As a professional photographer, it is important that you appear on photographic association lists in their "find a photographer" section. Many clients will log on to an association's web site as a way of prequalifying potential photography studios, so be certain that the information they will find there is correct. Photographers sometimes forget to pass on their new information when they change their e-mail or web address. Then, when a potential client tries to contact them via their links on the Professional Photographers of America (PPA) or Wedding and Portrait Photographers International (WPPI) sites, their e-mail is returned or they see a message that the web site cannot be found. Many clients will assume that you are no longer practicing photography and move on to another photography studio in your area. Make it a point to check your listings every month. It only takes a few minutes, but it can bring large dividends.

Check your listing often to be certain that the information is correct.

CREATIVE MARKETING WITH DIGITAL IMAGING

Instant Event Images. Besides traditional forms of marketing, digital imaging allows for some more creative marketing strategies. Many wedding photographers today now display images from the client's wedding on their notebook computer at the wedding reception itself. These photographers can create excitement about the images just taken hours or even minutes before and help build additional sales opportunities with guests viewing the photographs on the screen. The same idea is being utilized at other functions as well. Birthday parties, anniversaries, first communions, bar mitzvahs, etc., can all be marketed live to the guests in this manner.

Vendor Images. Wedding and event photographers can further benefit by providing digital image files to other related vendors, such as reception halls, caterers, florists, etc. Many of these vendors need quality images of their product or service for their marketing pieces and web sites. E-mailing files or sending a vendor a CD will help to promote goodwill with that vendor, and it will certainly result in more business leads. As a photographer, the cost involved is negligible, but the possible returns are immense.

Business Portraits. Business portraits have been revolutionized with digital imaging. Now, the client who is in a hurry for a 4x5-inch head shot for a newspaper can come in for the session, view the images, make a selection, and leave with the image on a CD. Some of our clients are having us e-mail images directly to the publication that needs the image. It is quick, efficient, and easy money. Everyone is so happy with this new technology because of the speed and quality that most of our business portrait clients now expect this level of service. If a studio cannot make imaging this efficient, they probably will not get the assignment at all.

Creating Marketing Pieces. Another advantage of digital imaging is that we are now able to create all of our own studio marketing pieces in-house without having to pay a typesetter. Using Adobe Photoshop, we can lay out and arrange our photographs and set type in a few minutes and send the printer-ready digital files to the printing company on a CD or even via e-mail. If we only need a few copies of a particular piece, we can even print it out ourselves on our Epson 2200 printer.

Promotional piece, Rice Photography.

■ MARKETING CHILDREN'S PHOTOGRAPHY

In today's competitive environment, photography studios need to create products and services that will set them apart from other studios. In the field of children's portraits, most of the major discount and department stores offer inexpensive photography for young children. We've all seen the offers—"Get 105 photos for only $9.95!" It is suicidal to try to compete with these discounters on price alone. These stores use their photography departments as a "loss leader" to get customers into their stores to buy other products.

Most photography studios offer portraiture of children as part of their services. The problem is this: to the consumer, professional photography studios offering children's portraiture do not seem all that much different from the department stores—other than the fact that they are much more expensive. If the consumer cannot see a significant difference in the product being offered, there is no reason for them to make the extra investment with the professional studio.

We established our Klassic Kids photography sessions as a way of setting us apart from both the department stores as well as other professionals in the area. Our Klassic Kids plan offers more than just great photos of our clients' children. As the name implies, we offer a classic style of portraiture that clients cannot receive from other photographers. By keeping the backgrounds simple and tasteful, utilizing specific props and antiques that truly add to the feel of the portrait, and using specialized clothing for our subjects, we can offer a one-of-a-kind portrait experience. Since our children's portraits are so different than what other studios and department stores offer, we can charge more money for the sitting and the finished prints.

The service that we provide has a much higher perceived value to the consumer, which helps us to stand out from everyone else. Our clients have had a very positive response to this style of children's portraiture. Our principle market has been the children of couples whose weddings we photographed. Since these couples are already familiar with the studio and our work, it is an easy sell and helps us to build clients for life.

Image by Mark Bohland.

On the following page is a promotional piece for this program.

◼ ENGAGEMENT SESSIONS

The bride and groom's engagement photograph is a long-standing tradition in most families. For years, couples have announced their impending nuptials with a notice in the local newspaper and an image of the happy couple. While many photographers charge a fee to couples for this portrait session, we include it free in some of our photography packages. At our studio, we refer to this offer as a "complimentary engagement session."

Our choice of words is very important. Because the session is complimentary, it has no cash value and cannot be exchanged for any other product or serv-

"Klassic Kids" Children's Portraits

Remember those special times in your child's life forever with a Klassic Kids portrait session from Rice Photography. Our exclusive Klassic Kids portrait session will record the innocence of childhood like no other studio. A perfect child's portrait takes considerable skill and planning. The portrait is meant to show expression and mood. No gaudy props. No all-white backgrounds. Our portraits are fashioned in simple and realistic settings. Specialized backgrounds, antiques, and timeless clothing add to the creation of a one-of-a-kind portrait that you will treasure for a lifetime. These heirloom-quality images can be in color, black & white, or antique sepia tones.

At Rice Photography, you are assured the best in your child's portrait. Patrick and Barbara Rice have each received national acclaim for their artistry in photography. They are both sought-after photographic instructors and each hold the Master of Photography and Photographic Craftsman degrees from the Professional Photographers of America.

Children grow up, but our portraits are forever. Call Rice Photography today at 555-555-5555 to schedule an appointment for our one-of-a-kind Klassic Kids portrait of your child.

Klassic Kids—Children's Portrait Prices

Package A—$380.00
- Up to four different poses
- 12 units total
- Additional units $25.00 each

Package B—$280.00
- Up to three different poses
- 8 units total
- Additional units $30.00 each

Package C—$160.00
- Up to two different poses
- 4 units total
- Additional units $35.00 each

Session fees are $40.00 for one child and $15.00 for each additional child. A package unit consists of your choice of one 8x10-inch print, two 5x7-inch prints, or eight wallet-size prints. All units must be from the same pose. Additional poses can be added for $15.00 each. Single units can be purchased for $44.00 each.

Klassic Kids—Children's Album Plan

You'll Receive:
- Up to four personalized portrait sessions over two years to record the changes in your child
- Klassic Kids photo album cover with two pages for photographs
- One 8x10-inch custom print from each session to be included in your child's Klassic Kids album
- One complimentary 16x20-inch wall print after completion of the fourth Klassic Kids portrait session
- Klassic Kids album plan members receive a 20 percent discount off any print packages and any additional photographs

All for only $189.00

ice. In actuality, the couple receives a free sitting in our photo studio. An on-location sitting is available at an additional fee. The couple views each of their images immediately after the session on our computer monitor. Because these sessions are digital capture, there are no film or proofing costs involved. The images are imported into Fujifilm's StudioMaster PRO software and the couple can then make their selections for reprints.

It was the engagement sessions that were the first area of our portrait business to become completely digital capture. Our very first Canon D30 camera more than met our expectations for this type of photography. Today, this may be the couple's first real experience with professional digital photography. It gets them accustomed to digital capture and we routinely answer any questions and concerns about the technology at this time. It also allows us the opportunity to get to know the couple a little more than we could have from the booking consultation alone.

Having a complimentary engagement session is a great marketing tool.

Having a complimentary engagement session is a great marketing tool that pays dividends in two ways. First, it can give you a competitive advantage over a studio that does not offer this type of service. Second, you can generate hundreds of dollars in image sales that you would not have had without the session.

When a couple schedules their complimentary engagement session, we send them out an information sheet that explains the session and the fact that they will view and choose their images immediately, as well as a brochure that explains how to dress for a portrait session. This simple mailing has answered many of the couple's questions and prevented misunderstandings about what kinds of services we provide.

Below is a promotional piece for this program.

Your Complimentary Engagement Session

At Rice Photography, many of our wedding photography packages include a complimentary engagement session. We use this session to get you "warmed-up" to the idea of professional portraiture for your wedding day. Not all of our couples choose to take advantage of this complimentary session. The session has no cash value and you can not receive anything in exchange for not using this session. Think of it like staying at a hotel that offers a complimentary continental breakfast with your stay. If you choose not to take advantage of it, you do not get money off your hotel bill or a voucher toward another meal. It is the same with our studio.

Your complimentary engagement session will be photographed digitally. This technology allows us to immediately show you the photographs recorded in the session. You should be prepared to allow about fifteen minutes to select any photographs you may want from the session at this time. You will view all of the images from the session on our computer screen in our studio. There are no paper photographs, printouts, floppy disks, or CDs to take home.

You are under no obligation to purchase any of the images. However, if you choose to wait and return for a second viewing of the digital images, there is a $25 service charge. All photographs ordered from your session are usually available in 2–4 weeks from the session date. If you have any questions, please call us at 555-555-5555.

Image by Jeff Smith.

Increasing Your Income to Balance Your Costs, by Jeff Smith

If you aren't currently using digital, you're probably getting the feeling that there's much more work involved in digital than with film—and you're absolutely correct. So, why would you go through all that extra work if you didn't see the opportunity for additional profit? When most photographers make the change to digital, they basically do exactly what they've always done with film. Why, then, would you want to incur the extra expense and work? Because of the lure of technology. We photographers are gadget freaks. We like to have an arsenal of toys, and there's no bigger toy on the market right now than the digital camera and the support system that goes with it. We all know the artistic possibilities of digital, but few people have figured out how to make the additional profit to cover those new expenses. If you make the switch to digital without formulating a clear plan to increase your profit line, you'll have less free time and less profit than you ever did with film—and you'll be in over your head after just one year.

After we made the decision to start offering digital sessions, we had the digital rep from our lab come to our studio to help in the transition. As we were going over the basics of how we'd configure the computers, handle the client files, etc., he asked me how we were going to show our clients the previews of their sessions. I explained that we'd show the clients their images and have them order immediately following their sessions. He looked at me with one raised eyebrow and explained that most photographers send in the files to have proofs made for clients. I told him that was exactly why I was going to show the previews after the session. When it comes to increasing your profit, take at look at what the average photographer is doing, then do something else. Why? Because many photographers would rather live in near poverty than learn to become more than what they are.

Selling after the session works in our studio for a number of reasons. First, we explain to each client, right from the beginning, what a digital session is. We explain that digital makes it possible to offer additional clothing changes, add special effects, and use templates. We also explain that they will be viewing and ordering from the previews after the session is over.

At our studio, the sales average achieved by digital sessions is twice that produced with film. Since no previews leave the studio, 100 percent of our orders from digital sessions come from our in-studio preview sessions. With film sessions, on the other hand, a good number of clients' names are given to collection agencies. Why? Because they never returned their costly take-home proofs. Taking this risk not only reduces the average sale, it also ensures that we won't get any business from younger siblings when they need senior portraits.

Selling After the Session. When selling portraits immediately after the session, you invest more time in the whole digital process, but it is time well spent. To make the selling process run smoothly, you'll need to develop a logical way to guide your clients through the buying process.

Image by Jeff Smith.

They will need to understand what they should do through each step of the procedure.

We have taken the same sales system we used with families (Trans-Vues projected into an empty frame) and modified it to work with digital. At our studio, we first sell the pose, then the size. To make this work, you need two things: the largest monitor you can afford and a program that will allow you to quickly display all of the images and the image names/numbers, making the image selection process easy both for you and for your client.

We use a 21-inch monitor for showing our images. Although I'd like to use a digital projector and have preview rooms set up like we used to for families, with our volume that would be impossible. We use a program called ImageBook that allows us to set up 16x20-inch "pages" and stamp each image with its file name so we can easily record a client's favorite selections.

We take about forty digital images (we shoot five photos for each of eight distinct backgrounds/poses). When it is time for the client to view the images, we open each file. For each image group, we decide which of the five images is best. This narrows forty images down to eight. Eight is the ideal number for us, because we sell so many folios, which have eight openings.

While the employee at the computer is pulling up the single files, a salesperson takes the clients to a private sales area, explains the packages, and helps the client decide on the one that's right for them. Since we can't show their portraits in wall-portrait sizes on the monitors, sample prints in various wall-portrait sizes are hung in each sales area. Once they decide on the package, they are brought back into the computer salesroom. The computer person then simply fills the packages with the eight images that are on the screen.

We have divided the sales areas because of our volume. If someone is taking a long time to decide on a package, they aren't taking up time at the computers, so we can start with someone else. The average order takes about 45 minutes, but some clients take up to an hour and a half. We had one senior who brought in both her mom and step-mom, and they spent two-and-a-half hours ordering. It was a long time, but the sale was over $1,500.00! Everything is measured in terms of time versus money. If someone has the money, I have the time!

Setting Up Your Viewing and Sales Station. Immediately following the session, the clients are brought to the preview area. Our goal here is to get them through this area quickly. We provide no seating in this area. Why? Because people make decisions faster when standing than when sitting. When someone is seated they want to relax and chat. When they're standing, they want the process to move along quickly so they can sit.

When we get our clients into the preview room, the first thing we explain is how easy it is to select the best pose, telling them, "There is always one image that's by far the best in each image group (pose/background combination)." This

Image by Jeff Smith.

way they don't question themselves endlessly, thinking the decision is a hard one to make.

We do provide seating in the sales area, which is where the client will select their package. It takes more time for the client to figure out which package they'll buy. We do ask that all of our clients make a list of all the people they'll be giving a portrait to before they come in for their session; we've found that it speeds up the process.

When the client has decided on a package, they return to the previewing room to put the individual poses into it. We have computers in some of our sales areas just in case we get backed up in the previewing room.

Supportive Service. Selling after the session only works if you take the appropriate steps and guide your client through the buying process. You're a professional. Your clients look to you for help in every aspect of taking the photographs. It's only natural for them to look to you and your staff to help them through the buying process as well.

Since professional photography is a higher ticket item than mall or department store photography, our clients need to know what to expect. Many photographers like to surprise clients with the price of their portraits, but it's better to prepare them for what's ahead. Inform your clients that they'll be viewing and selecting their portraits right after their session. Tell them that packages range in price from "X" to "Y," and that they'll need to put down your standard deposit to start an order.

Once you've given your clients the information they need to make informed decisions, they'll find this type of selling very personal and much easier than taking proofs home (where they don't have professionals to help them). Every past client who has gone through this process after a digital session has told us that it was a pleasant experience, and the vast majority commented on how much easier it was than using proofs.

They'll find this type of selling very personal and much easier than taking proofs home.

■ A PROFESSIONAL PERSPECTIVE
**Marketing During the Transition to Digital—and Beyond,
by Jeff and Kathleen Hawkins**

There was a time when digital photography represented low-end, quick-turnaround photos. Technology has improved and times have changed; if your clients want superior photographs, they hire a photographer who can offer a state-of-the-art digital experience. In order to introduce your market to the digital age, you have to prepare them for this style of imaging, sell them on the advantages of the technology, and adapt new selling techniques into your studio's routine.

Remember, you may be excited about your new camera and your new process, but your excitement may not be reassuring to your clients. Your new style may actually scare your clients away rather than attract them to you—especially if you are not careful with the wording you use.

Image by Jeff Hawkins.

Beginning the Transition. Begin this marketing transition indirectly, by introducing your digital images to your clients. In the beginning, your clients do not necessarily have to know what type of camera you are using. Before beginning this transition, did you feel compelled to educate them on your Hasselblad or the model of Nikon you were using? Most likely, you did not—it may have even annoyed you when they asked. If that's the case, why should the digital experience be any different? Once you feel comfortable enough with the camera, manipulation, and printing techniques to create high-quality images, start showing different options at bridal shows and in your advertising.

At this point, people will begin to take notice of your innovative product. You will have captured their attention without necessarily having mentioned the word "digital" in a sales presentation. You are selling the results, not the jargon. Once you have begun to prepare your portrait and wedding clients, begin educating the local vendors on the benefits of your studio's new technology. As a suggestion, send out an e-mail or a press release. You might consider wording your release as demonstrated in the following example:

With our recent purchase of the latest state-of-the-art digital technology, Jeff Hawkins Photography can now offer you and your clients more!

- Need stock photos right away? Give us a call!
- Want to make your advertisements unique? Give us a call!
- Your brides will benefit, too, with online ordering, reception displays, and much more!

Once you have begun the basic education and preparation of your market, you have begun the selling process. In order to successfully sell your work in the digital age, you should begin marketing in four fundamental stages. Perfecting these four marketing stages will assist your business in learning how to work full-circle. These stages include: pre-interview, consultation, wedding day, and post-wedding day.

Stage One: The Pre-Interview. The first stage is the pre-interview phase. This phase actually begins the moment you initiate preparing the community for the digital transition your business is endeavoring. Begin by showcasing a variety of digital images on your web site, in your brochures, and in your publication advertising. For example, consider displaying a watercolor image, a sepia print, and an image with special effects or photo enhancements. Create a brochure that highlights some of your new features. Begin distributing this brochure to vendors and at bridal shows. Be sure to submit stock photos to area publishers and vendors to be used in exchange for photo credit. This is essentially free publicity. It is not very time-consuming and is extremely cost-effective. Brides will begin to notice your work all over town—your name should be everywhere they visit!

Continue to take advantage of the convenience of today's technology and contact the publishers of local media. There are many wedding-industry publications that can assist you in getting your name out into the community.

However, advertising alone does not make the most effective use of your dollars. Working the contact lists these publications provide you with is also crucial. (These lists contain the names, wedding dates and contact information for people who expressed interest in your ad and requested additional information.) In these days of electronic media, it is very effective to request your leads via the Internet. To avoid getting all your leads at once and not having enough time to effectively follow up with them, request that your leads be e-mailed to you on a weekly or biweekly basis. Next, delete the leads for the dates you are no longer available. The main information that you will need to print will include: name, address, e-mail address, and phone number. Narrow your listing to the above items and print them on mailing labels.

At that time, you should prepare an e-mail (see samples below and on the next page). Save this "form letter" and personalize it for all the leads generated. This should be an introductory letter and should include your web site address in the first paragraph. Including your web address will create a link for the prospective clients and make it easier to view your work. If you receive twenty leads a week, after deleting the dates you are not available, it should only take a few minutes to respond with an e-mail to your prospective clients. This places your company in front of most of your competition.

Lastly, use the printed address labels to send promotional postcards or brochures to clients—especially those who did not list their e-mail addresses. Typically, we prioritize sending brochures to prospects whose wedding dates are in months we want or need to book. Then, we send postcards to contacts whose weddings are in less crucial months.

We prioritize sending brochures to prospects whose wedding dates are in months we want or need to book.

Sample E-mail—Letter of Introduction

Subject line:
Please visit www.jeffhawkins.com

Body:
Jeff Hawkins Photography wants to be more than just your wedding photographer; we want to be your family photographer. All of our couples receive customized pricing levels, unlimited time and images, online ordering, and a Lifetime Portrait Program membership! Featuring the work of an industry-sponsored, international award-winning photojournalist and published author, our studio offers clients all the latest technology. We create more than images—we create art! Let us capture your emotions, feelings, and relationships and document them for a lifetime. Remember, your wedding memories are not expensive, they are priceless! Do not hesitate to call, as dates do book up rather quickly!

Best wishes,
Kathleen
Jeff Hawkins Photography
(555)555-0000

Stage Two: The Interview. The second stage in the selling process—the interview—may very well be the most crucial. Your client has seen your work, spoken with you over the phone, and is now ready to make a decision about hir-

Sample E-mail—Letter of Introduction

Subject line:

Please visit www.jeffhawkins.com

Body:

We recently received your wedding request and wanted to assist you as quickly as possible. We would love to work with you! I know that selecting a photographer can be an overwhelming experience. Let me help make this choice a little easier for you.

Top Ten Reasons to Book Jeff Hawkins Photography Today

1. You'll receive a free Master File CD-R of all your images with the purchase of a Premier or Deluxe album. This is safer than negatives, which may scratch, bend, or be misplaced! With it, you can e-mail images to friends or archive your family heirloom.
2. You can become a member of our Lifetime Portrait Program.
3. We have an innovative pricing structure that gives you the most flexibility in purchasing what you want. Let the pictures determine the size of the photos—not the package! Typically, our custom levels begin at $2,500 and our intimate weekday weddings begin at $750. Each can be customized for your needs.
4. We use state-of-the-art technology featuring top-of-the-line 35mm, medium format, and digital camera equipment! Not to worry—we always come prepared with plenty of backup equipment!
5. All of our couples receive a slide show display of their images to showcase at the reception. You select the size of the display: 15-inch laptop display, television, or LCD projector and screen.
6. Don't stress if you have a blemish on your special day—with state-of-the-art computer technology, Jeff Hawkins will eliminate any imperfections, creating images you will cherish for a lifetime.
7. When you hire Jeff Hawkins Photography, you hire Jeff Hawkins! You don't have to worry about a stranger photographing your important moment! Plus—as a double bonus for you—you will always have the benefit of having his highly trained assistant(s) on hand. This means we can be in two places at once, if needed!
8. All of our couples receive online ordering. This makes your life simpler and easier, since you won't need to lug heavy proof books all around town! You can even direct all of your friends and family to your special web site with your private password.
9. With our state-of-the-art technology, our brides receive digital proofing. With no image limits, our average wedding day capture ranges from 500 to 1000 photos! This means you get complete coverage.
10. You are not alone in designing your album. We care about the quality of our product and realize this is most likely the first album you have ever designed—so we won't leave it all up to you. All of our couples receive an album design consultation session, walking you through the design process. You'll leave the session with a computer printout of what your final product will look like! It is our goal to have your album designed and into production within two weeks of your special day. This is a family heirloom; let us help you make a storybook, not a scrapbook!

I look forward to the opportunity to speak to the two of you and hope to hear from you soon. If you would like to quickly review our work, our web site is located at www.jeffhawkins.com. Furthermore, you can also preview our work in both *Orlando Bride* magazine and *The Perfect Wedding Guide*.

Please contact me at (555)555-0000 or (555)555-0001, if you have any questions or concerns—or to schedule your consultation. Remember, your wedding memories are not expensive, they are priceless! We hope to hear from you in regard to your wedding photography. Do not hesitate to call, as dates book up rather quickly!

Sincerely,

Kathleen

Jeff Hawkins Photography

ing your services. This is the most important stage of the money-making process. At this stage, what you say may not be as important as how you say it. Consider these digital blunders:

Image by Robert Kunesh.

BLUNDER: "We are a proofless studio!"

BETTER: "Our state-of-the-art digital technology allows us to offer you more convenient proofing methods. All of our clients receive three different proofing options. You will receive online ordering for your family and friends; three duplicate digital proofing DVDs (one for you and for each set of parents to keep); and a professionally-bound contact sheet with each edited image numbered for reference. This means you don't have to worry about lugging around or shipping heavy proof books! Our couples find this to be easier and more convenient."

Implying that you are "proofless" is like telling the clients that they receive less with you than with photographers who use traditional proofs. You do use proofs, you just don't use paper proofs. Doesn't the second option sound more appealing than the first? With this improved presentation, it appears as though your clients are receiving more, thus increasing the value of your studio's work.

BLUNDER: "We are completely digital!"

BETTER: "Our studio uses state-of-the-art technology. As an award-winning artist, our photographer will use whatever camera is most appropriate for what is being photographed. Don't worry, we have plenty of backup equipment! That is one of the main benefits to hiring an experienced studio."

Again, doesn't the second option sound more appealing? Unfortunately, many couples have been misinformed by people or bridal publications about digital imaging. They believe that you are using the same digital camera as their Uncle Bob. If you have backup equipment, the above statement is 100 percent accurate. If something should happen and the digital cameras are not working properly, then we would switch to a film camera. Although you may be completely digital 99 percent of the time, by selecting your wording carefully you can overcome potential objections about camera selection and backup equipment. The key is to overcome the objection before the client even asks the question!

BLUNDER: "Oh, I can have that done in a minute—I'll just print it out on my printer!"

BETTER: "Let me see what our production schedule looks like and how quickly we can get that into processing. I will do my best to get the order processed as quickly as possible for you."

Clients still find comfort in knowing their images went through a magical chemical process. The easier it seems for you to produce their print, the more you reduce the value of your image. If an expedited process is required, state that you have made an exception in the workflow (and never get it done too quickly). It may only take a few minutes to create a driver's license photo, but it takes longer than that to create a work of art!

As the quality of printers rises and the cost falls, clients are increasingly

Image by Jeff Hawkins.

familiar with (and in ownership of) these high-quality items. Therefore, it is best not to reveal too much information about the printers you use. Leave these specifications unstated unless a client should directly ask for this information. Make sure you also address the issue of archival quality, even if the client doesn't ask about it. This helps to convince clients that they could not create an identical image themselves. Your entire process from image capture to presentation should be a magical work of art—a special talent that only you possess!

After the client has had the opportunity to complete our client questionnaire and interview sheet, we explain the top ten reasons why people hire Jeff Hawkins Photography. This information is also included on our brochures and on our web site.

In order to develop your own "top ten (or three or five) reasons" list, you'll need to stop and carefully evaluate your competition. When we created our list,

Address the issue of archival quality, even if the client doesn't ask about it.

there were essentially three photographers in our area who created healthy competition. One was very good, but very inexpensive. One was priced right, but gave away the negatives and had a cookie-cutter approach to the albums. The other was a popular studio, but farmed out the clients to other photographers in the area.

Next, analyze what makes your studio unique. For example, our studio has more technology and equipment than any of our competitors. Second, Jeff has an exceptional ability to blend traditional, photojournalistic, and photo-relationist photography. Finally, we have a variety of customer service–oriented systems and procedures in place. However, ours is probably one of the most expensive studios in town.

Before (above) and after (right) images by Jeff Hawkins.

After analyzing the above considerations, we knew what objections we would need to overcome and what we needed to sell in every interview. Many photographers like to believe their images sell themselves, but unfortunately they don't. Rather, the client has to accept and believe in the perceived value of your product. This can be achieved in the following manner:

Image + Money = Perceived Value

Based on this idea, the top ten reasons we developed are listed below and are discussed with clients at the beginning of every interview. Also included are statements called "trial closes." These are all designed so the client can hardly help but answer yes, geting the client ready to say yes to the big question—the decision to sign a contract with you. Reviewing each of these "reasons" helps us to head off potential objections from our clients and sets us apart from our competitors by educating the consumer as to what makes us unique. These benefits are always discussed before price is even mentioned!

These benefits are always discussed before price is even mentioned!

1. We have no time limits, image limits, or set packages.
This statement tells clients that we don't believe in the cookie-cutter approach to wedding photography. We will photograph as many images as needed and personalize their coverage time and product to their specific event.

Image by Penny Adams.

Image by Jeff Hawkins.

TRIAL CLOSE: Do you see how, since your day starts at "X" o'clock and ends at "X" o'clock, that extra time can benefit you?

2. We have a new and innovative pricing structure.
This lets clients know we offer flexibility—the ability to purchase what they want. Each level of coverage is customized to fit the couple's unique needs. They may want quality and not necessarily quantity, or they may be real picture people. We have so much confidence they will love the images, that it makes no difference whether they hire us at the basic level and buy à la carte for the album images, or whether they choose a much higher level of coverage.

TRIAL CLOSE: How big of a "picture person" would you say you are?

3. With the purchase of a Premier or Deluxe album, our clients receive their images archived on a CD.
We let clients know that this CD is much safer than negatives, which may scratch, bend, or be misplaced. Many of our clients use the images as screensavers, in thank-you notes, or even to e-mail images to family and friends. They can use the CD to print very small images, but we let them know that we take their images through about four more professional processing steps. Therefore, I always encourage our clients to continue to have their professional images printed through the studio—but the CD is great to have for archival purposes!

TRIAL CLOSE: Do you have access to a computer? Can you see the importance of both of us having a backup copy of such an important family heirloom?

4. You do not have to worry about perceived imperfections on the day of the wedding!
Since we take each image through a digital conversion process, our brides don't

have to worry about having unwanted blemishes, exit signs, and other distracting elements appear in their photographs.

TRIAL CLOSE: Can you get excited about being able to remove unwanted exit signs or blemishes?

5. When you hire Jeff Hawkins Photography, you hire Jeff Hawkins.

We let our clients know that they don't have to worry about a stranger photographing them on their important day. Plus, as an added bonus, they know Jeff will always have at least one (often two) highly trained assistants with him. Because of this, our brides know that we can literally be in two places at once, if needed.

TRIAL CLOSE: Can you see the value of knowing who you are going to be working with prior to the wedding day and knowing that they will not be working alone?

6. We always come prepared with plenty of backup photography equipment.

We use state-of-the-art technology with top-of-the-line 35mm, medium format, and digital camera equipment.

TRIAL CLOSE: Doesn't it make you feel comfortable to know that we will come prepared with more than one camera—just in case it is needed?

Image by Jacob Jakuszeit.

7. With our state-of-the-art technology, our brides receive an "Image Reflections" display to showcase at the reception, plus digital proofing.

This makes our clients' lives easier and saves them money. With no image limits, we shoot an average of 500–1000 images per wedding, so the client gets complete coverage.

Image by Jacob Jakuszeit.

TRIAL CLOSE: Wouldn't you rather have the problem of having too many images to select from than not enough? Don't you think your parents would appreciate being able to select from traditional color images as well as the artsy images you enjoy?

8. We offer online ordering.

All of our couples receive online ordering. This makes their lives much simpler by eliminating the need to lug heavy proof books all around town. Instead, the couple can simply direct their friends and family to a special web site. With a unique password assigned to the couple, the site can only be accessed by the people they want to see their photos.

All of our couples receive an album design consultation session.

TRIAL CLOSE: Wouldn't you rather send your friends and family a note with a web address instead of having to ship proof books all around the country and collect their orders? You don't have to be the middle man—let them come directly to us to place their order.

9. You are not alone in designing your album.

We care about the quality of our product. We realize that their wedding album is most likely the first album our clients have ever designed—and that can be stressful. Therefore, we don't leave it all up to them. All of our couples receive an album design consultation session, during which we walk them though the design process. It is our goal to have their album designed and placed into pro-

duction within two weeks from their special day. After the design session, the couple leaves our studio with a computer printout of what their final product will look like. This is a family heirloom—we can help them make a storybook, not a scrapbook.

TRIAL CLOSE: Do you see the importance of using the photographs to capture a story like this book did?

10. We understand the importance of developing a relationship with our clients.

We do not just want to be our clients' wedding photographer, we want to be their family photographer. All of our brides receive an honorary membership to our Lifetime Portrait Program. With their membership card, for the rest of their lives (or ours), they can come in and receive complimentary pregnancy, baby, family, business, or graduation sessions—all the important moments in their lives! (Dates, times, and locations are subject to availability.)

TRIAL CLOSE: Do you plan to have children someday? Well, there is no expiration date on this offer. We want to be able to make a children's album for you one day, as well. Typically, the fees run from $200 to $350 for each session, depending on the image type and number of people that are photographed. These sessions would now be free to you. Of course, you can add à la carte items from there!

We understand the importance of developing a relationship with our clients.

When we finish discussing this list, it's time for the final trial close: Based on the services and quality of photographs, can you see the benefit of hiring Jeff Hawkins Photography? The client's answer: "Yes!" Your response: "Great! There's only one question, then—what level of service do you want? We understand the importance of quality and can also respect your finances. We want you to have a high quality product and will work with you in every way possible. These are your choices . . . (list options). Which would be better for you?" Then, go for the close and get the retainer.

Stage Three: Wedding Day Marketing. You sold your services, but the marketing should not cease the day of the wedding. You can now make the digital difference and generate a refreshing amount of excitement about your

Image by Jeff Hawkins.

images. This is done by promoting your online image ordering to guests, by creating an image display at the reception, and by selling pre-reception parent and bridal-party gifts.

As previously suggested, creating an online ordering system is indisputably the best way to profitably capitalize on the flow of traffic onto your web site. The online ordering process consists of two steps. First, be sure to distribute online

ordering cards on the wedding day. Second, when the images are ready for viewing, be sure to follow up with a letter to the bride and her attendants that provides a link to your web site and instructions for viewing their special images.

Begin marketing the reception image display during the interview. This is an inexpensive way to increase the perceived value of your services. The client has three display options for their images: a laptop, an SVHS-compatible television (if provided by the venue) or an LCD projector and screen. If the LCD projector is provided by us, rental and setup charges will apply. However, if the LCD projector and screen are provided by the client, there is no additional charge.

To create the slide show, follow the steps listed below. Typically, the slide show setup begins at the start of the first course of the dinner. Your goal should be to have it running by the time the meal is complete.

Image by Robert Kunesh.

1. Turn on the laptop.
2. Insert your media device (i.e., microdrive, CompactFlash card) into the PCMCIA card.
3. Insert it into the computer PC card slot located on the side of the laptop.
4. Create a folder with the client's name on both the FireWire drive and the computer's hard drive.
5. Copy the images from the media card to the new folder. (Important! Use the copy command, not the move command! That way, if there is a failure or a computer glitch, you will not lose any files and the images are protected twice.)

6. Once the images are copied, open the folder in a viewing program—such as ACDSee.
7. Quickly edit the images, removing any photos where the subject blinked, there are exposure problems, etc.
8. As necessary, rotate images in the hard drive folder into a vertical orientation.
9. Begin the slide show by clicking the slide show button located on the menu bar.

It is best to run the slide show without music—you don't want to compete with the entertainment. This is just a continuous display for people to enjoy. The

bridal couple will love to see their special images—it's instant gratification. As they watch, the bridal party and guests become more animated. After all, everyone loves to be seen on the big screen! For elderly people, who are often tired and have had a long day, this also provides an entertainment option other than dancing. They usually watch in awe of the technology.

Next to the images display (which we call our "Image Reflection" display), include an assortment of online ordering cards. Make sure these cards are styled to appear as gifts from the bridal couple, and not as a blatant publicity piece from your company. This helps maintain your upscale appeal.

At least a week before the wedding, be sure to promote a custom-framed gift collection. Consider the following suggestions to up your sales.

For example, you can create a "Daddy" frame. (We find the Art Leather large Futura frames in wine, silver, or onyx are the most popular choice.) This gift is purchased prior to the special day. Give the bride a gold, silver, or bronze pen and let her personalize it for her father. Keep the mat in the frame box and bring it to the reception. Next, select one of the photographs from the father/daughter formals or the father/daughter dance. During the reception,

The bridal couple will love to see their special images—it's instant gratification.

when you have taken all the dance images you can tolerate, print out one of these images at a 5x7-inch size on your printer. We have found it much easier to delegate this task to an assistant, but have also managed to find the time to do it ourselves when needed. Trim this photo and place it into the frame, then drop it into a gift bag with tissue paper. In order to present their special gift at the reception, we have established a minimum purchase of three frames. This covers the cost and time of setting up the printer and preparing the client's special gift on-site.

When the bride is ready to exit, have her signal you to get the gift and photograph the presentation. You have now increased your sales with the $100+ purchase of the framed image and by creating additional images for the wedding album. These images could include: bride giving gift to Dad, Dad opening gift, Dad with tears in his eyes, Dad hugging daughter, Dad holding the frame with daughter and son-in-law. This idea also works well for multiple presentations to both sets of parents, siblings, the maid of honor, etc. Bridal party folios are also big sellers.

Finally, if the couple is on a budget and elects not to purchase a gift collection, think about contacting one of their parents or the bridal party members and selling them a large Futura or Deluxe Futura frame. Create a signed mat and print an 8x10-inch family portrait or bridal party portrait for them to take on their honeymoon. This is just one way to let the couple know that they will be thought of while they are away!

Keep in mind, this production should be done behind the scenes. No one needs to know how long it takes or how difficult it is to create your work of art. Famous chefs wouldn't reveal their secret recipes, so why should you? Keep in mind the following suggestions:

1. Take a detailed order prior to the wedding day: note who the gift is going to,

Image by Patrick Rice.

what type of product will be delivered, photojournalistic style or traditional, etc.

2. Prepare the images in a separate room with quality lighting.

3. Bring a print cutter! Trying to cut small images with scissors will slow you down tremendously.

4. For optimum effect, have your product ready for delivery an hour before the wedding's end.

These are just a few examples of how, with digital technology, you can now offer more, advertise more, and make more money!

Stage Four: Post-Wedding-Day Marketing. To capitalize on the advertising gain of promoting our online images at the wedding and to draw traffic to our web site, we have created a post-wedding-day marketing program. This increases web site activity, educates consumers about our services, and increases our sales.

We include in our basic-level service a program called "20/20 Vision." This is a customer-service program that gives clients a minimum of twenty images online and twenty online image cards to distribute in thank-you notes to guests who were unable to attend. These images are on display within the first week after the wedding date. Often, our clients visit Internet cafes on their honeymoon to get a sneak peek at the images from their special day!

Once the couple designs their album and picks up their proofing CD/DVD, they have the option of purchasing a program to display all of their images online for up to sixty days.

Image by Jeff Hawkins.

DIGITAL ALBUMS

In the wedding photography market, we closely watch all trends and new products that are introduced to our industry. As a photographic judge for both PPA and WPPI, I am afforded the opportunity to see some cutting-edge photography and image presentations. A few years ago, I began seeing wedding albums created by the Australian company Digicraft. Their books were unlike anything that I had ever seen—they were truly remarkable! In album competition,

Digicraft digital album cover.

Digicraft digital album with images by Barbara Rice.

Digicraft digital album with images by Barbara Rice.

their books dominated the competition, winning every major award in photographic competition. More importantly, I saw this product as something that my upscale wedding clients would be interested in owning.

At a WPPI convention, I had the opportunity to spend some time with Alex, one of the owners of Digicraft. Alex explained his company's commitment to creating the most unique wedding books anywhere. At his booth, I was able to see more of these albums that so impressed me in competitions. Soon, we decided to offer their product line to our customers.

After we received our own sample book from a wedding that my wife Barbara had photographed, all we had to do was begin showing this new digital album to our clients. The response has been truly amazing! Everyone is absolutely overwhelmed by the artistry of the book. These albums redefine the wedding album industry. The creative possibilities with digital albums are endless. Each book is a unique work of art. There are no templates, so no two albums will look the same.

The books are a sizeable investment for the wedding photographer—a cost that we pass along to our clients. It is interesting that when we first began offering this book, all of my colleagues felt that it was too expensive and we would never sell any of these albums. This has not been the case. Yes, the books are expensive, but some of our clients have been more than happy to make the additional investment in a truly one-of-a-kind wedding album. These books literally sell themselves. Even the clients who cannot afford our Digicraft albums still

admire and desire them. To me, this is the key. I want our studio to offer that spectacular book that sets us apart from the competition.

Digicraft digital album with images by Barbara Rice.

Working with Digicraft is much easier than I would have expected, given the fact that they are in Australia. We simply send them a CD of the images we want to be included (via Federal Express or Airborne Express), and they take care of the rest. We like to give very general instructions so as not to limit the creativity of their design staff. We split the images up into folders that will each represent a two-page spread when you view the book. We also include any text that should be included (sending this as a Microsoft Word document) and allow them to create the design.

In only a few weeks, we receive a PDF file via e-mail that shows the entire book design—page by page. If any changes are necessary (there usually are not), they can be made at this time before the book is printed and bound. About a month later, the book arrives at our doorstep ready for the client to pick up.

The ease of using this product has really eliminated a lot of labor hours for our business. We don't incur the time or cost involved in sending images to our lab. We also don't have to stock album pages or mats. Each book is custom printed by Digicraft, and the savings in time more than offsets the expense of the book.

THE FUTURE

The Doctrine of Small: Pre-dicting the Fall of Mom-and-Pop-Studios, by Micheal Dwyer

In my columns for photography magazines, I've gone to great lengths to convince photographers that the times they are a'changin'. I've tried to convince you that while the battles are many, if you're balanced, focused, and take small steps, you'll be fine. Perhaps I was too optimistic. I'd like to tell you of a revolution I see on the horizon that will be even larger than the digital revolution. One with much deeper roots and far greater conse-quences: While the digital revolu-tion simply changes the way we capture, sell, and deliver images, this new one will change the very structure of our businesses.

How many of us are old enough to remember when going out to eat was a big deal? Mom and Dad packed the kids into the Buick and away we went to Joe's Diner or Mabel's Steak House.

Image by Bernard Gratz.

The family probably ate for less than $10. Ahh, the good old days.

Well, is either Joe's or Mabel's still around?

Are any of the restaurants where you and your family ate this week family-owned? Or are they part of a chain or franchise? OK, forget about restaurants—

how about motels, banks, gas stations, grocery stores, or furniture stores you frequent? How many of those businesses that were once operated by a mom and pop are operated now by a CEO and a board of directors? Do you see the analogy coming? Look carefully at those industries. Many are not dominated by huge multinational conglomerates but by small, regional companies with very focused products and services.

Few photographers, including me, have any interest or need to compete with "mart" portrait studios. With all due respect, they're the McDonalds of the portrait industry. But like those other businesses, the mom-and-pop portrait industry will have to wage battle just to survive.

How do we survive in a culture where our clients are ever more mobile and ever more fickle, in a heavily advertised market with shrinking margins, and in a climate of revolution? Digital imaging is not the end but the means. It's not the war but the weapon that is changing the battlefield. Digital tools change our strategy and determine who can and who can't win this war. I see two major fronts.

First, to a great degree, digital imaging changes the point where the value of your product is identified. In a film studio, it all happens in front of the camera with the click of the shutter. The expression, background, exposure, lighting, and relationships are present at that moment. In a digital studio, all that stuff can

Image by Scott Gloger.

be enhanced, even completely changed later, by the photographer or someone else. Digital imaging brings the opportunity to add value to your images long after the exposure is made. That's huge.

A film studio sells prints. A digital studio sells prints and services. These services can be standardized and effectively managed on a larger scale than was possible when everything happened in the camera room. It's a different paradigm.

Second, digital imaging has a great power to teach. Train a photographer in a film studio, and it will be a week before you know if he's on the right track or if he's screwed it up. With a digital file, you know instantly. You can train, critique and approve, all within seconds, while the client is still in front of the camera. Digital imaging lowers the risk of having someone besides mom or pop behind the camera. It's another huge paradigm shift.

Together, these two changes lead to a business model in which success is less dependent on one great photographer and more on great businesspeople.

Image by Jacob Jakuszeit.

I can hear you saying, "Yeah, but that's not for me. No one can produce the kind of images I can." Yes they can. Having made the transition into being a fully digital, multiple-photographer company, I can tell you honestly that our photography is clearly the finest it's ever been. More important, it gives me the opportunity to teach, empower, and leave a legacy in our studio and our business that will outlast me. There are young people begging for the opportunity to learn what you know. Great leaders and great businesspeople will incorporate that into a very successful business model—yours or theirs.

How Digital Images Change the Art of Management. Digital imaging requires studio owners to manage to a degree we haven't had to before. To manage technology, to manage workflow, to manage financials, to manage people. In his book *The Seven Habits of Highly Effective People* (Simon & Schuster, 1990), Dr. Steven Covey makes a great point: "You manage things, you lead people." Studios with just two or three people and annual sales of less than $250,000 find this especially hard—too much stuff in too many specialized areas for two or three people to handle. The expense and intricacy of digital imaging is driving studios that can't or won't reinvent themselves out of business.

In the vacuum that remains, studios that evolve will be bigger, faster, and stronger. Like the restaurants, banks, TV stations, and grocery stores that survived thirty years of change, these studios understand how to manage. All have embraced technology. All understand workflow and systems. All have accurate, up-to-date financial statements. Many operate in multiple locations. Most have annual sales in excess of $1 million.

Three caveats here. As in the other industries, none of this happened overnight for the studios. It's a long drawn-out process that happens over as many as ten years. But most of the photographers I know would like to be around for at least that long.

In the Midwest anyway, small towns are still insular. Many still have mom-and-pop restaurants. But clearly we don't have the number or variety we once had.

And finally, using the restaurant analogy, many upscale restaurants are still mom-and-pop operations, and that can go for studios as well. Businesses that are highly specialized and stylized and have the market to support their niche may be somewhat immune to this revolution, but the principles of good business, effective marketing, and sound management still apply.   Image by Mark Bohland.

FINAL THOUGHTS

Regardless of how much you may resist it, change is inevitable.

Film is not dead. However, film is becoming a less practical way for photographers to record images of their clients. In much the same way, the old 4x5-inch Speed Graphics of the 1950s didn't go bad or stop working; photographers chose to make the transition to 120 roll film with those new-fangled Hasselblad and Mamiya cameras of the 1960s. Then, in the late 1980s, wedding photography was turned upside down with the trends toward photojournalistic coverage and those 35mm autofocus cameras. I remember when photographers told me they would never use that small format film. Eventually, almost every wedding photographer was using a Nikon or Canon 35mm auto-everything camera with those amazingly fast lenses.

It is no different with digital imaging. The cameras will continue to get better, and possibly even less expensive. Manipulation software can now do things that we didn't even dream of just a few years ago. Both Kodak and Fuji have realized and accepted the challenge of digital imaging and are making both hardware and software to make our lives easier.

So, what does all of this mean to today's portrait and wedding photographer? First of all, regardless of how much you may resist it, change is inevitable. Unless you are planning on retiring or finding another line of work, you will have to embrace digital imaging in the very near future. As a photographer, you can choose to be a leader in this exciting digital world or you can choose to try to play catch-up with all of us when you are inevitably forced to make the transition. As you've seen throughout this book, the obstacles to digital have been almost entirely overcome—and there are a multitude of advantages to be gained. As a result, there's never been a better time to make the change!

INDEX

By the Same Author...

PROFESSIONAL PHOTOGRAPHER'S GUIDE TO
Success in Print Competition
Patrick Rice

Learn from PPA and WPPI judges how you can improve your print presentations and increase your scores in competition. $29.95 list, 8½x11, 128p, 100 color photos, index, order no. 1754.

Infrared Wedding Photography
Patrick Rice, Barbara Rice and Travis Hill

Step-by-step techniques for adding the dreamy look of black & white infrared to your wedding portraiture. Capture the fantasy of the wedding with unique ethereal portraits your clients will love! $29.95 list, 8½x11, 128p, 60 b&w images, order no. 1681.

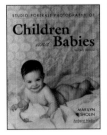

Studio Portrait Photography of Children and Babies, 2nd Ed.
Marilyn Sholin

Work with the youngest portrait clients to create cherished images. Includes techniques for working with kids at every developmental stage, from infant to preschooler. $29.95 list, 8½x11, 128p, 90 color photos, order no. 1657.

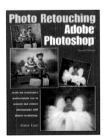

Photo Retouching with Adobe® Photoshop® 2nd Ed.
Gwen Lute

Teaches every phase of the process, from scanning to final output. Learn to restore damaged photos, correct imperfections, create realistic composite images, and correct for dazzling color. $29.95 list, 8½x11, 120p, 100 color images, order no. 1660.

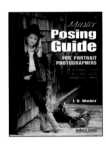

Master Posing Guide for Portrait Photographers
J. D. Wacker

Learn the techniques you need to pose single portrait subjects, couples, and groups for studio or location portraits. Includes techniques for photographing weddings, teams, children, special events and much more. $29.95 list, 8½x11, 128p, 80 photos, order no. 1722.

High Impact Portrait Photography
Lori Brystan

Learn how to create the high-end, fashion-inspired portraits your clients will love. Features posing, alternative processing, and much more. $29.95 list, 8½x11, 128p, 60 color photos, order no. 1725.

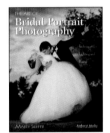

The Art of Bridal Portrait Photography
Marty Seefer

Learn to give every client your best and create timeless images that are sure to become family heirlooms. Seefer takes readers through every step of the bridal shoot, ensuring flawless results. $29.95 list, 8½x11, 128p, 70 color photos, order no. 1730.

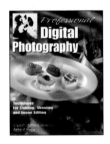

Professional Digital Photography
Dave Montizambert

From monitor calibration, to color balancing, to creating advanced artistic effects, this book provides those skilled in basic digital imaging with the techniques they need to take their photography to the next level. $29.95 list, 8½x11, 128p, 120 color photos, order no. 1739.

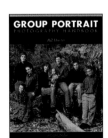

Group Portrait Photographer's Handbook
Bill Hurter

With images by top photographers, this book offers timeless techniques for composing, lighting, and posing group portraits. $29.95 list, 8½x11, 128p, 120 color photos, order no. 1740.

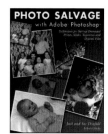

Photo Salvage with Adobe® Photoshop®

Jack and Sue Drafahl

This book teaches you to digitally restore faded images and poor exposures. Also covered are techniques for fixing color balance problems and processing errors, eliminating scratches, and much more. $29.95 list, 8½x11, 128p, 200 color photos, order no. 1751.

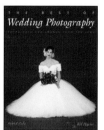

The Best of Wedding Photography

Bill Hurter

Learn how the top wedding photographers in the industry transform special moments into lasting romantic treasures with the posing, lighting, album design, and customer service pointers found in this book. $29.95 list, 8½x11, 128p, 150 color photos, order no. 1747.

The Best of Children's Portrait Photography

Bill Hurter

Rangefinder editor Bill Hurter draws upon the experience and work of top professional photographers, uncovering the creative and technical skills they use to create their magical portraits. $29.95 list, 8½x11, 128p, 150 color photos, order no. 1752.

Web Site Design for Professional Photographers

Paul Rose and Jean Holland-Rose

Learn to design, maintain, and update your own photography web site. Designed for photographers, this book shows you how to create a site that will attract clients and boost your sales. $29.95 list, 8½x11, 128p, 100 color images, index, order no. 1756.

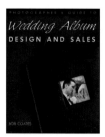

PHOTOGRAPHER'S GUIDE TO
Wedding Album Design and Sales

Bob Coates

Enhance your income and creativity with these techniques from top wedding photographers. $29.95 list, 8½x11, 128p, 150 color photos, index, order no. 1757.

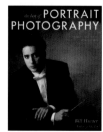

The Best of Portrait Photography

Bill Hurter

View outstanding images from top professionals and learn how they create their masterful images. Includes techniques for classic and contemporary portraits. $29.95 list, 8½x11, 128p, 200 color photos, index, order no. 1760.

THE ART AND TECHNIQUES OF
Business Portrait Photography

Andre Amyot

Learn the business and creative skills photographers need to compete successfully in this challenging field. $29.95 list, 8½x11, 128p, 100 color photos, index, order no. 1762.

Creative Techniques for Color Photography

Bobbi Lane

Learn how to render color precisely, whether you are shooting digitally or on film. Also includes creative techniques for cross processing, color infrared, and more. $29.95 list, 8½x11, 128p, 250 color photos, index, order no. 1764

The Best of Teen and Senior Portrait Photography

Bill Hurter

Learn how top professionals create stunning images that capture the personality of their teen and senior subjects. $29.95 list, 8½x11, 128p, 150 color photos, index, order no. 1766.

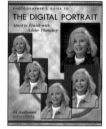

PHOTOGRAPHER'S GUIDE TO
The Digital Portrait

START TO FINISH WITH ADOBE® PHOTOSHOP®

Al Audleman

Follow through step-by-step procedures to learn the process of digitally retouching a professional portrait. $29.95 list, 8½x11, 128p, 120 color images, index, order no. 1771.

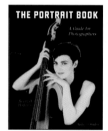

The Portrait Book

A GUIDE FOR PHOTOGRAPHERS

Steven H. Begleiter

A comprehensive textbook for those getting started in professional portrait photography. Covers every aspect from designing an image to executing the shoot. $29.95 list, 8½x11, 128p, 130 color images, index, order no. 1767.

Professional Strategies and Techniques for Digital Photographers

Bob Coates

Learn how professionals—from portrait artists to commercial specialists—enhance their images with digital techniques. $29.95 list, 8½x11, 128p, 130 color photos, index, order no. 1772.

By Contributors to This Book . . .

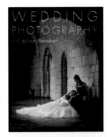

Wedding Photography with Adobe® Photoshop®

Rick Ferro and Deborah Lynn Ferro

Get the skills you need to make your images look their best, add artistic effects, and boost your wedding photography sales with savvy marketing ideas. $29.95 list, 8½x11, 128p, 100 color images, index, order no. 1753.

Professional Marketing & Selling Techniques for Wedding Photographers

Jeff Hawkins and Kathleen Hawkins

Learn the business of wedding photography. Includes consultations, direct mail, advertising, internet marketing, and much more. $29.95 list, 8½x11, 128p, 80 color photos, order no. 1712.

Professional Techniques for Digital Wedding Photography, 2nd Ed.

Jeff Hawkins and Kathleen Hawkins

From selecting equipment, to marketing, to building a digital workflow, this book teaches how to make digital work for you. $29.95 list, 8½x11, 128p, 85 color images, order no. 1735.

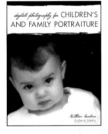

Digital Photography for Children's and Family Portraiture

Kathleen Hawkins

Discover how digital photography can boost your sales, enhance your creativity, and improve your studio's workflow. $29.95 list, 8½x11, 128p, 130 color images, index, order no. 1770.

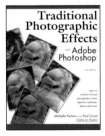

Traditional Photographic Effects with Adobe® Photoshop®, 2nd Ed.

Michelle Perkins and Paul Grant

Use Photoshop to enhance your photos with handcoloring, vignettes, soft focus, and much more. Every technique contains step-by-step instructions for easy learning. $29.95 list, 8½x11, 128p, 150 color images, order no. 1721.

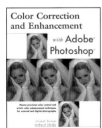

Color Correction and Enhancement with Adobe® Photoshop®

Michelle Perkins

Master precision color correction and artistic color enhancement techniques for scanned and digital photos. $29.95 list, 8½x11, 128p, 300 color images, index, order no. 1776.

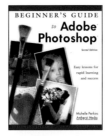

Beginner's Guide to Adobe® Photoshop®, 2nd Ed.

Michelle Perkins

Learn to effectively make your images look their best, create original artwork, or add unique effects to any image. Topics are presented in short, easy-to-digest sections that will boost confidence and ensure outstanding images. $29.95 list, 8½x11, 128p, 300 color images, order no. 1732.

Posing for Portrait Photography

A HEAD-TO-TOE GUIDE

Jeff Smith

Author Jeff Smith teaches sure-fire techniques for fine-tuning every aspect of the pose for the most flattering results. $29.95 list, 8½x11, 128p, 150 color photos, index, order no. 1786.

Corrective Lighting and Posing Techniques for Portrait Photographers

Jeff Smith

Learn to make every client look his or her best by using lighting and posing to conceal real or imagined flaws—from baldness, to acne, to figure flaws. $29.95 list, 8½x11, 120p, 150 color photos, order no. 1711.

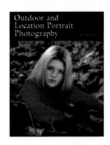

Outdoor and Location Portrait Photography 2nd Ed.

Jeff Smith

Learn to work with natural light, select locations, and make clients look their best. Packed with step-by-step discussions and illustrations to help you shoot like a pro! $29.95 list, 8½x11, 128p, 80 color photos, index, order no. 1632.

Professional Digital Portrait Photography

Jeff Smith

Because the learning curve is so steep, making the transition to digital can be frustrating. Author Jeff Smith shows readers how to shoot, edit, and retouch their images—while avoiding common pitfalls. $29.95 list, 8½x11, 128p, 100 color photos, order no. 1750.

Success in Portrait Photography

Jeff Smith

Many photographers realize too late that camera skills alone do not ensure success. This book will teach photographers how to run savvy marketing campaigns, attract clients, and provide top-notch customer service. $29.95 list, 8½x11, 128p, 100 color photos, order no. 1748.

Lighting Techniques for Low Key Portrait Photography

Norman Phillips

Learn to create the dark tones and dramatic lighting that typify this classic portrait style. $29.95 list, 8½x11, 128p, 100 color photos, index, order no. 1773.

The Best of Wedding Photojournalism

Bill Hurter

Learn how top professionals capture these fleeting moments of laughter, tears, and romance. Features images from over twenty renowned wedding photographers. $29.95 list, 8½x11, 128p, 150 color photos, index, order no. 1774.

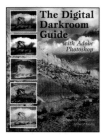

The Digital Darkroom Guide with Adobe® Photoshop®

Maurice Hamilton

Bring the skills and control of the photographic darkroom to your desktop with this complete manual. $29.95 list, 8½x11, 128p, 140 color images, index, order no. 1775.

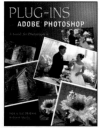

Plug-ins for Adobe® Photoshop®

A GUIDE FOR PHOTOGRAPHERS

Jack and Sue Drafahl

Supercharge your creativity and mastery over your photography with Photoshop and the tools outlined in this book. $29.95 list, 8½x11, 128p, 175 color photos, index, order no. 1781.

Power Marketing for Wedding and Portrait Photographers

Mitche Graf

Pull out all of the stops to set your business apart and create clients for life with this comprehensive guide to achieving your professional goals. $29.95 list, 8½x11, 128p, 100 color images, index, order no. 1788.

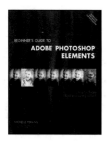

Beginner's Guide to Adobe® Photoshop® Elements®

Michelle Perkins

Take your photographs to the next level with easy lessons for using this powerful program to improve virtually every aspect of your images—from color balance, to creative effects, and much more. $29.95 list, 8½x11, 128p, 300 color images, index, order no. 1790.

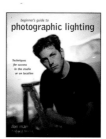

Beginner's Guide to Photographic Lighting

Don Marr

Create high-impact photographs of any subect with Marr's simple techniques. From edgy and dynamic to subdued and natural, this book will show you how to get the myriad effects you're after. $29.95 list, 8½x11, 128p, 100 color photos, index, order no. 1785.

The Portrait Photographer's Guide to Posing

Bill Hurter

Get the posing tips and techniques that have propelled over fifty of the finest portrait photographers in the industry to the top. $29.95 list, 8½x11, 128p, 200 color photos, index, order no. 1779.

Master Lighting Guide for Portrait Photographers

Christopher Grey

Efficiently light executive and model portraits, high and low key images, and more. Master traditional lighting styles and use creative modifications that will maximize your results. $29.95 list, 8½x11, 128p, 300 color photos, index, order no. 1778.